The Story of Silbury Hill

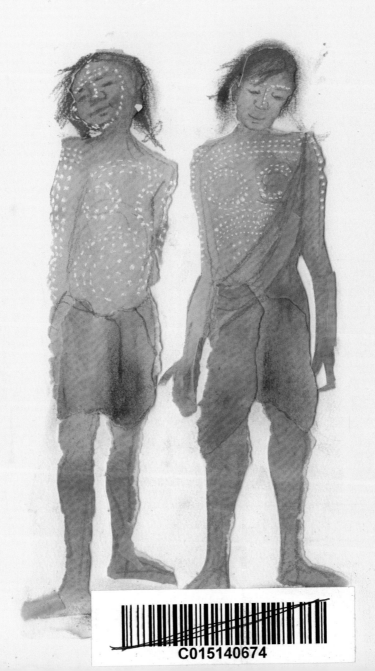

The Story of Silbury Hill

Jim Leary and David Field

With a foreword by Sir David Attenborough

And illustrations by Judith Dobie and Eddie Lyons

Published by English Heritage, Kemble Drive, Swindon SN2 2GZ
www.english-heritage.org.uk
English Heritage is the Government's statutory adviser on all aspects of the historic environment.

First published 2010

ISBN 978-1-848020-46-7

Product code 51528

British Library Cataloguing in Publication data
A CIP catalogue record for this book is available from the
British Library.

The National Monuments Record is the public archive of English Heritage. For more information,
contact NMR Enquiry and Research Services, National Monuments Record Centre, Kemble Drive,
Swindon SN2 2GZ; telephone (01793) 414600.

Brought to publication by Joan Hodsdon, Publishing, English Heritage.

Typeset in ITC Charter 9.5/16.1pt

Edited by Lesley Adkins
Indexed by Alan Rutter
Page design by Simon Borrough

Printed in Belgium by DeckersSnoeck.

Cover
Silbury Hill in the Moonlight.
© David Inshaw

Frontispiece
Silbury Hill viewed from alongside the Kennet stream just south-west of Avebury.
Photographer and figures unknown (BB81/2779).

'For a monument at Silbury Hill'

This mound in some remote and dateless day
Rear'd o'er a Chieftain of the Age of Hills,
May here detain thee Traveller! from thy road
Not idly lingering. In his narrow house
Some warrior sleeps below: his gallant deeds
Haply at many a solemn festival
The Bard has harp'd, but perish'd is the song
Of praise, as o'er these bleak and barren downs
The wind that passes and is heard no more.
Go traveller on thy way, and contemplate
Glory's brief pageant, and remember then
That one good deed was never wrought in vain.

Robert Southey, 1797

Contents

Foreword

There can be no doubting that the monuments left by our prehistoric past have a powerful hold on our imaginations. Can there be anyone who has walked, cycled or driven past the great mound of Silbury who has not wondered who constructed it, when and why they did so, and what lies within it – if anything – apart from chalk?

Television did its best to satisfy this appetite right from its early days in the 1950s. Initially it did so with archaeological quizzes and documentary films. But by the late 1960s it was sufficiently competent technically to contemplate what might well be considered the ultimate archaeological broadcast – reporting an excavation, not by displaying discoveries that were made days, weeks or months earlier, and certainly not by reburying objects and digging them up again to cries of feigned surprise, but having cameras at a site almost continuously so that discoveries could be seen as they were made. That way the public at large, in whose name the excavations are being carried out, could share in the genuine excitement of the excavators.

And that was what BBC2 aimed to do in 1968. The network was new, only the third in the country to take to the air. Its declared policy was to tackle new programme subjects and try new ways of treating them. So why not show a properly scientific excavation as it happened? Cameras could be at the site continuously, for long periods of time, so that they would be able to record and even relay crucial discoveries as they were made. If necessary, regular programme schedules could be interrupted to visit the site at key moments as they occurred, predictably or unpredictably. And what more exciting candidate could there be for such an excavation than Silbury Hill, looming large and mysterious beside the busy arterial road that ran from London to the West Country?

Right from the beginning, the network made it clear that it was not expecting or wanting a treasure hunt. Or at least, if it were, then the treasure it sought was information – information that could lead to an understanding of the motives of the builders when they started on the immense task of constructing the Hill. The press, of course, refused to accept such high-minded protestations. Would BBC2 be disappointed, they asked incredulously, if the excavators unearthed the golden horseman that, according to legend, lay at the Hill's heart? Of course not, the broadcasters said. There you are, said the press, it is a treasure hunt. And so when the first season came to an end and neither gold nor any other spectacular artefact had been found, the press declared the whole exercise a failure. BBC2 did not regard it as such. Millions of people, for the first time, had watched an excavation in detail as it proceeded and had been able to understand the complex techniques of modern archaeology.

The same could be said, of course, of the latest investigations which are described in this book. They did not unearth any material treasure either. But they made it possible to assess the discoveries made in the past and added more details to our knowledge and understanding of the Hill. In the end, one of the aims of archaeological investigation is surely to use material remains to construct an idea of what lay in the minds of men and women living long ago. So the final chapter of this book, like many of its kind, must be one that we write in our own minds. And Jim Leary and David Field have enabled every one of us to make that attempt with their lucid descriptions of the work of their predecessors and their own most recent investigations.

David Attenborough

Acknowledgements

Conservation work at Silbury Hill was one of the largest and most challenging of projects conducted by English Heritage during the early years of the 21st century. The project was managed by Rob Harding, while Amanda Chadburn, Inspector of Ancient Monuments, played a prominent guiding role and provided considerable support and encouragement throughout. Inevitably, a large number of individuals were involved, and among them the authors of this account played a major role in the archaeology and interpretation of the site. The monument and its environs were analytically investigated, surveyed and the documentary evidence assessed by David Field in 2001, while Jim Leary directed the excavations in 2007 and 2008. Various surveys, analyses and targeted excavations took place between these times, during which Niall Morrissey was Superintendent of Works. Fachtna McAvoy managed the excavations between 2000 and 2007. Professor Michael Worthington and Professor Richard Chandler provided superb advice regarding cavities within the structure of the mound, while Mark Kirkbride led the miners and engineers from Skanska. Initially Kevin Brown and later Bob Bewley, successive Regional Directors for English Heritage, headed the Project Board and were instrumental in moulding the form of the project.

We wish to thank all colleagues involved in the successful completion of this project, who participated in the various assessments, surveys and analyses leading up to the major intervention of tunnel re-entry in 2007–8, including Graham Brown, Bernard Thomason, Tom Cromwell, Mick Clowes, Matt Canti, Andrew David and Paul Linford. Special thanks, however, must go to the archaeologists, miners and engineers who worked in uniquely difficult conditions, both on the steep slopes and particularly within the tunnel – every one of them gave more than could be expected.

The on-site archaeological team comprised Dan Barrett, Tony Baxter, Kayt Brown, Paul Bryan, Gill Campbell, Matt Canti, Danielle de Carle, Liz Chambers, Eleanor Collier, James Cooper, Tom Cromwell, Foxy Demeanour, Dave Fellows, Dave Field, Susanne Geck, Nicola Hembrey, Ellie Leary, Jim Leary, Neil Linford, Paul Linford, Fachtna McAvoy, Louise Martin, Eloise Metson, Andy Payne,

Peter Popkin, Jenny Ryder, Duncan Stirk, Maria Vinnels and Fay Worley. The Skanska mining and engineering team consisted of Barry Carlin, Terry Hilton, Mark Kirkbride, Mick McCaffery, Vernon Nightingale, Bob Tutill and Colin Wilkinson. Arthur McCallum was the Clerk of Works from English Heritage and Susan Westlake assisted with on-site publicity.

Along the way large numbers of people helped in one form or another. Sarah May, Brian Kerr and Andrew David, all from English Heritage, provided guidance and managerial support during and after the fieldwork. The environmental team was managed by Gill Campbell, who also analysed the plant remains. Finds were managed by Nicola Hembrey and Kayt Brown. Matt Canti undertook the geomorphology of the old ground surface, Paul Davies analysed the land snails, Mark Robinson the insects, Barry Bishop the flintwork, Fay Worley and Ian Riddler the antler and Josh Pollard the sarsen stones. Deborah Cunliffe, Eddie Lyons and John Vallender produced illustrations at various stages of the project, and Judith Dobie's reconstruction illustrations, many of which are used here, proved invaluable in assisting with interpretation of the monument.

Members of the Avebury Archaeological and Historical Research Group provided stimulating discussion and advice. Among them were Josh Pollard, Mark Gillings, Martyn Barber, Andrew David, Peter Fowler, Gill Swanton, Kate Fielden and Brian Edwards. Both Kate and Brian are thanked, initially for keeping us on our toes but also for providing much insight and valuable historical research. Ros Cleal is thanked for the warm welcome, assistance and discussion at the Alexander Keiller Museum and, along with Nick Snashall and Gill Swanton, for archaeological and moral support throughout the period and particularly during the excavation (especially the welcome supply of tiffin from Ros), while spiritual support came in the form of Terry the Druid (Terry Dobney). Melanie Pomeroy (subsequently Pomeroy-Kellinger), formerly World Heritage Site Officer for Kennet District Council and latterly Wiltshire County Archaeologist, is also thanked, along with her successor at Kennet, Sarah Simmonds.

Several TV companies filmed on site, but LionTV on behalf of BBC4 were present on site for much of the summer of 2007, and although it is never easy balancing the sometimes conflicting demands of filming schedules with on-site work, Chris Corden, George Williams (both Directors) and Alice Robinson (Researcher) made filming considerably more bearable than it would otherwise have been. Pre-Construct Archaeology Ltd provided two site staff at very short notice. We are most grateful to the family of Ken Wilson for use of part of his poem; to Virginia Zimmerman for her transcription of Emmeline Fisher's poem and useful notes on it; and to the Drax family for use of the portrait of Edward Drax and to Jason Bowerman for facilitating this.

We would like to warmly thank all those whose discussions have helped shape this book. David Field would particularly like to thank Pete Glastonbury, Julian Cope and others for the privilege of endless discussions waiting for our children outside the school gates. We would like to thank Martyn Barber, Mark Bowden, Brian Edwards, Jonathan Last, Sarah May, David McOmish and Pete Topping who kindly read through the manuscript and commented on the text, while individual chapters were commented on by Gill Campbell, Matt Canti, Tom Cromwell, Rob Harding, Neil Linford, Pete Marshall, Arthur McCallum and Tony Wilmott. We are grateful to Joan Hodsdon and Robin Taylor for guidance during the production of the book, and also to Lesley Adkins, whose hard work considerably improved the text. David Collison is thanked for his helpful recollections of the 1960s work, and Peter Fowler for his thoughts on the rate of vegetation growth on chalk. We would also like to thank David Attenborough for kindly writing the Foreword and David Inshaw (www.tabretts.co.uk) for allowing us to reproduce his painting 'Silbury Hill in the Moonlight' for the cover. We are particularly indebted to David and Richard Hues and the National Trust for access, and to Lord Avebury, the owner of Silbury.

Finally, we would both like to thank our long-suffering spouses and offspring, and it is to them that this book is dedicated: Christine Cox and Catherine Cox-Field for patience during countless walks around the Silbury landscape, and the latter, then at Avebury school, for providing a different perspective on the text; and Ellie Leary for her support and helpful comments on draft chapters, and daughter Dora, who was born during the writing of this book and did so much to slow progress. Sprocket the Scottish deerhound was present throughout much of the fieldwork and made the Silbury site office a better place to work.

Introduction

Silbury Hill is one of Europe's best-known monuments. It has survived for millennia, anchored in position as time passed it by, barely touched by the events that have shaped the British Isles. It was standing there in 1643 when the Royalists swept past from Oxford on their way to the great Battle of Roundway Down, during the English Civil War. Before that it had stood throughout the reign of Henry VIII, when Jane Seymour was living at Wolfhall in the nearby Pewsey Vale. Going further back in time, nearly a millennium ago, the Battle of Hastings is a recent event compared to the founding of Silbury Hill. Indeed, this great artificial mound, the largest in Europe, was already ancient when Vikings fought it out with Saxons at nearby East Kennett and when the great Wansdyke, a huge defensive bank and ditch that stretches across much of the Marlborough Downs, was constructed along part of the skyline to the south of the mound. Earlier than the Vikings and Saxons, Roman surveyors used Silbury Hill as a sightline to lay out a road, the forerunner of the A4 that still links London with Bath, and they may have used the summit to set up their instruments, so Silbury has subtly influenced the changes in the landscape that surrounds it.

But we need to go back even further in time to find the origins of Silbury Hill, because the Roman invasion in AD 43 stands less than halfway in time between the creation of the mound and now – back through the Iron Age, when Oldbury Castle, now a series of grass-covered earthworks on Cherhill Down, was a hive of activity, and further back through the Bronze Age, when many of the round barrows were constructed. There, poised after the Stone Age and before the Bronze Age, just when the first metals were appearing in England, was the point at which Silbury Hill began its incredible story.

The mound in question lies within a UNESCO World Heritage Site that incorporates the world-famous Stonehenge, as well as the internationally important and well-known Neolithic Avebury henge, stone circles and stone avenues, the Windmill Hill causewayed enclosure, the West Kennet chambered long barrow and a number of other contemporary monuments. Each of these sites is notable in its own right, but they take on additional significance when considered as part of a greater complex.

Situated prominently alongside the London to Bristol highway, it is no wonder that Silbury Hill attracted early interest. Much comment and discussion will have been lost to us, but the visit of so illustrious an individual as King Charles II in 1663 brought the monument to the attention of the antiquarian community. This is where we start the story of Silbury Hill: the account of antiquarian and archaeological obsession, of the trenches, shafts and tunnels dug into it, and of the modern collapses they led to. The story continues with the events that followed a calamitous occurrence in 2000, as well as the difficulties of steering a path through the arguments and wrangles of different interest groups, the investigations into past activities and the excitement of archaeologists as they were able to investigate the interior of the mound. It is also the story of these new archaeological investigations, and the fresh understanding these excavations have given us about its creation and development in the Neolithic period, and of how the Hill was seen by later communities during the Roman and medieval periods, right up to the modern day.

This is the story of Silbury Hill; more precisely, it is our story of Silbury Hill. For we are acutely aware that, like all historical accounts, archaeology can produce its biases and prejudices. It presents our interpretations, our thoughts, our insights, and for this we make no apology. That is, after all, the way interpretation works and hypotheses are developed. The book has been written by two of the archaeologists most closely involved with the project; people who actually worked on the hill; with dirt under their fingernails; were, at times, blinded by rain while surveying the mound, slipping and sliding with every step; and who toiled in the foul and sweaty tunnel for months. This is our account of Silbury; ancient and modern.

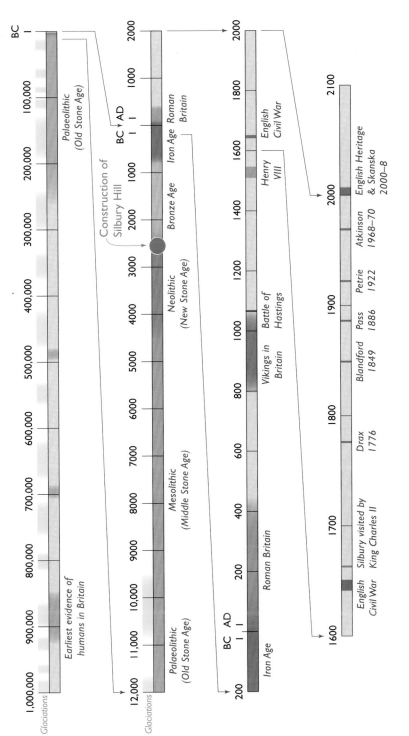

Timeline to show the position of Silbury Hill in the past.

1 The nature of time

Millions turned out and stood along the banks of the River Thames in London to celebrate the arrival of the year 2000. Far upstream, close by the Swallowhead spring, one of the sources of the great river overlooked by Silbury Hill, similar though more subdued celebrations took place. In the capital city, for several hours leading up to the midnight hour, people streamed out of the tube stations and filtered into various vantage points by way of restaurants, public houses, clubs, discos and other venues. At times, the human current from the Strand was so strong that people were carried bodily around the flanks of a tightly packed Trafalgar Square into an equally overcrowded Whitehall.

The whole of London, probably the whole of Britain, the western world, at least those who followed the Christian calendar, seemed to be on the streets. As Big Ben struck the hour and thousands of bottles of champagne were opened, an enormous firework display began along an eight-kilometre stretch of the river bank. Wave after wave of colour co-ordinated explosions – green, indigo, cerise – that could be appreciated by looking into the far distance or close up. The pièce-de-résistance, said to represent a ribbon of fire, waterfall or sheet of light along the river itself, failed somewhat but, overwhelmed by the display, few noticed or cared.

Many partied all night, either out on the streets or after returning to clubs and hostelries. As the crowds slowly began to disperse, champagne bottles lying in the gutter popped one after another as ambulances and police cars eased their way slowly through, crushing them and sending showers of glass flying across pavements at ankle level. Monitored by mounted police, an enormous crowd gathered outside Waterloo Station and waited patiently for two hours or more to be compressed and funnelled through the entrance in order to begin the journey home.

Some 120km towards the river source, locals at Avebury in Wiltshire considered the prehistoric earthworks and stone circles of the great 4,500-year-old henge a more appropriate place to mark the event and to contemplate the passage of time. Unlike the orange glow that constantly masks the night sky in the capital, here one can see the stars and appreciate the importance of the night sky and its relationship with the land. On this occasion they were supplemented by a host of humanly created stars, supplied from rockets, mortars and Roman candles. There was over-enthusiasm here also, of course, as one individual let off a huge explosion on nearby Waden Hill. The bells of St James rang and were joined in the distance by those belonging to other communities. No crush here, people just went home to their houses and farms. Aside from the occasional rustle in the hedgegrows as badgers scavenged around their territory and deer searched for anything green, peace returned to the countryside. As it had done for millennia, water sparkled and emerged from the local springs, then carved a careful course through valleys and hills, past fields and villages; increasing in volume and gathering speed towards the great metropolis of London on its timeless passage to the sea.

The passage of time

The passage of time had been a common theme during the preceding year. Writers and television programme makers had considered the process, our modern perception of it and how it had been captured and measured. Calendars, clocks and other timepieces all came under scrutiny, as did the industrial perception and use of time, whereby the value of labour could be calculated and used as a commodity, and the compilation of complex train timetables that allowed for the passage of time itself. A preface in all this, but almost written off as irrelevant to the 21st century, was an acknowledgement of an earlier way of life; one based on agriculture and the land, where natural cycles, the seasons, lunar periods, the soil and the weather played a more central role in everyday life. Those working on the land did not need to know whether it was seven o'clock or eight o'clock on Tuesday 30th or Wednesday 31st, only whether there was enough light to see and if the weather was fine enough to ripen the crops.

To mathematicians and scientists, not to mention archaeologists and historians – those for whom the passage of time is of some academic importance – the celebrations came too early as they did not mark the transition from one millennium to another but the beginning of the year leading up to it. Prehistorians in particular, who increasingly rely on scientific dating techniques, are used to being as precise as they can about time periods. But objections were lost amid a popular clamour to mark the magic year 2000, and of course archaeologists

Silbury Hill covered in snow. (AA000901)

missed the point by not realising that it was the symbolism of the number that was important. In contrast, others saw the event in a completely different way, some prophesying doom and disaster as Armageddon approached.

There were new resolutions, new starts, new challenges, but around Avebury little changed in the first few weeks of the year 2000. As they had always done, the springs around Silbury Hill continued to feed the great river system, while the timeless agricultural calendar progressed, and people gathered at Avebury for Beltane on 1 May – a festival traditionally marking the beginning of summer and widely observed by the pagan community. Increasing numbers of travellers and supporters of alternative religions had been attending such events since the late 1990s, and for many this marked the start of a series of summer festivals, and gatherings that would culminate in attendance at the 30-year-old Glastonbury Festival in late June. This year David Bowie, the Chemical Brothers, Travis, Rolf Harris and Burt Bacharach (the latter eventually pulled out) had been booked to headline the weekend of music and other activities, and good crowds were expected.

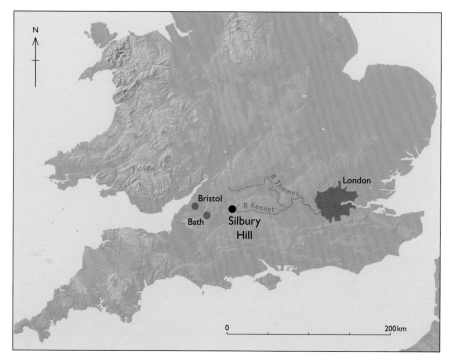

Map showing the location of Silbury Hill.

The Hill and the hole

However, an astonishing event marked the new millennium in Wiltshire and set the backdrop for the summer. Towards the end of May tourist numbers at Avebury were high for the Spring Bank Holiday weekend, and on Monday 29th a visitor sightseeing in Wiltshire ventured up the enormous earthen mound of Silbury Hill. The monument is often said to be the largest humanly constructed mound in Europe, and indeed the large flat-topped conical mound is of great proportions, some 31m high and surrounded by a wide ditch that extends in the west to form a sub-rectangular 'tank' or cistern that is often flooded in winter. The mound is a Site of Special Scientific Interest due to the rarity and diversity of the chalk grassland and wild flowers, and consequently access is discouraged. However, two causeways across the ditch make access to the mound an easy matter, and the anonymous visitor crossed one of these and scaled the steep slope. On reaching the summit he immediately noticed that something was wrong; very wrong. There was a gaping hole in the top.

On being informed, Chris Gingell, archaeologist and property manager for the National Trust at Avebury, rushed to the site, climbed the steep slope and gazed in astonishment. There was indeed a hole, a large one, some 2m across and a good 12m deep. There had been an unusual amount of rain in Wiltshire that month which had perhaps affected stability. Could it be that parts of the summit were unstable? Chris recalled that a shaft had been dug into the mound during the 18th century, although little was known of it, but in any case the immediate concern was for public safety. The hole constituted a hazard of the first order to unsuspecting tourists who disregarded advice about climbing the Hill. Extremely concerned, he informed English Heritage, and then arranged to stay on the summit overnight to ensure that no-one fell in.

The great mound known as Silbury Hill, a site of international renown, is situated in the heart of the North Wiltshire Downs and has for long proved to be an archaeological enigma. While certainly among the earliest of archaeological sites to be recorded and commented upon, its sheer bulk has provided difficulties and challenges to investigation. It was only during the late 1960s, when an extensive campaign of excavation by the late Professor Richard Atkinson featured

Aerial photograph of Silbury Hill taken in 2000, showing the hole on the summit. (NMR 18745/11)

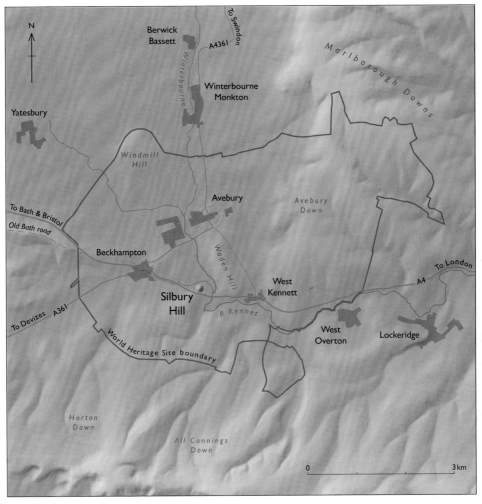

Map showing the location of Silbury Hill within the Stonehenge, Avebury and Associated Sites World Heritage Site.

as the first televised archaeological excavation, that evidence of its true date was finally revealed. The programmes were watched by well over a million people, enthralled by the possibility of witnessing a discovery to rival that of Tutankhamen. Even then, the mound's purpose was widely assumed to be that of a burial mound, with some important person at its heart. No evidence was found to support such an idea, and this inability to provide clear answers about the mound's purpose has allowed an air of mystery to persist, encouraging a flood of alternative explanations based on a recipe of mysticism, metaphysics and myth. In the past the mound has been variously considered to cover the body of a royal person, to be a temple to Mercury, to be the motte of a castle, a constituent part of the Avebury ritual complex, a mound for assemblies and law making, a platform for astronomical observations, for Druidical sacrifice and for beacons. It has been thought to be dedicated to the sun, to represent the earth, or to be Cludair Cyvrangon, where assemblies of Welsh legend were held.[1] Today, it is sometimes thought of as the centre of the spiritual world, a fixture in countless ley-line based theories, the navel of the earth goddess or an image of her, a harvest hill,[2] a hill altar or Mother Hill;[3] in other words, a focal point for alternative beliefs. Set alongside this, conventional archaeology might appear rather sedate and even boring, but, as often proves to be the case, the facts as revealed by excavation are of far greater interest, excitement and fascination.

It is important, however, to recognise that Silbury Hill and its adjacent monuments have a long history and that categorising them as 'Neolithic' simply isolates and focuses on a snapshot from their past; an essential picture perhaps, but one that ignores much of their subsequent change and development. It is quite possible that the very first activity on the site dates back to an even earlier time, while 4,000 years of erosion, modification, building and other activities have certainly taken their toll. In other words, the monument that we see today is the current manifestation of many periods of activity and weathering processes and not the form intended by the original builders. The same process can be observed in the parish church of St James in Avebury, where the long and short stone work at the junction of nave and tower proclaim it as an 11th-century church, while roundel windows set high up in the nave walls confirm its ancestry. However, the first feature to greet the visitor is not of this date but a decorated 12th-century Norman doorway leading to a 15th-century aisle. In fact, much of the visible building is of this date; nevertheless, while it is largely obscured, evidence of the original Saxon build can still be sought out and observed.

Archaeological earthworks are also like this, the product of millennia of activity and land-use – of decay, change, addition and erosion. They represent what in archaeological jargon is called a palimpsest – that is, multi-layered traces of past activities, with the earliest still discernible. Like the origin of the church, details of the initial structure can be traced, but the later fragments need to be carefully peeled away and interpreted in order to understand it. There is a further twist. Hidden away in the external fabric of St James, at the junction of the nave and tower, is a fragment of a decorated Saxon cross. Such crosses were used as focal points for the new Christian religion before the construction of church buildings, and the presence of such a feature here is important, for it demonstrates that the struggle between new and old beliefs in Avebury pre-dated the construction of the church. Similar devices can sometimes be used in the analysis of earthworks to demonstrate land-use and how archaeological sites developed over time.

Silbury past and present

There is rarely a day when the viewing area of Silbury Hill is completely bereft of visitors. Even Christmas Day sees a straggle of enthusiasts studying the interpretation panels. Although access to Silbury Hill itself is discouraged, visitors are nevertheless attracted from all over Britain and all over the world to observe its great bulk from the viewing area. Some are local, from the nearby villages of Winterbourne Monkton, Berwick Bassett, East Kennett and Yatesbury or from Avebury itself, who perhaps wish to keep in touch with an important component of their childhood landscape. Many are from more distant places, the Netherlands, Japan, Canada, and either think it a curiosity worth a few minutes' stop on the tourist trail from London to Bath, or consider it a world-famous archaeological site that merits a longer visit. Others, having made a pilgrimage from cities and towns around the country, treat the encounter as a deep experience, the mound being considered the 'omphalos', navel or centre of the spiritual world; or a sacred 'eye', or a pregnant earth goddess.[4] Most require car parking facilities (few arrive by bus), toilets, sustenance and explanation (usually in that order) and seek answers in the National Trust's Alexander Keiller Museum at Avebury. Others require somewhere to camp and cook, while the monuments themselves provide both solace, meaning and spiritual comfort, and the Henge Shop provides a range of literature to satisfy the intellect.

In fact, it may be that as many people make the pilgrimage to the site today as ever did in the past. While certainly an archaeological monument of first importance, whatever its original purpose, part of its present significance is as a modern temple. While these extremes may be stereotypes, they serve to emphasise the variety of individuals who visit the monument and their equally wide array of expectations. They also place centrally the problematical question of how our foremost prehistoric monuments should be managed and presented. Just how much concrete, how many car parks, ice cream/hot dog stalls, hotels and so on should there be? Like Stonehenge, Avebury has even received past mention of its own by-pass. The matter also applies to the monuments themselves and to what extent they should be conserved, repaired, managed or reconstructed. After all, they are the way they are because of millennia of decay and addition.

It was not always this way. Despite lying immediately adjacent to the A4, London to Bristol road, Silbury Hill formerly received comparatively few visitors. John Leland passed by in about 1540 and noted that the River Kennet rose at Silbury Hill Bottom 'where by hathe be[en] camps and sepultures of men of warre'.[5] William Camden, topographer and historian, also stopped to record the source of the river:

> the River Cunetio, in the Saxon tongue Cynetan, commonly Kenet, ariseth neere unto a litle Village of the same name, which some would have to bee that Cunetio mentioned by Antoninus, but the distance of both sides gain-sayeth it. Here Selburie, a round hill mounted up aloft to a great height, which by the forme of the hill it selfe and the outward setling of the earth, may seeme to have bene cast up by mans hand ... I am of opinion rather that this of Selburie was set there in stead of a limit, if not by the Romans, then certainly by the Saxons.[6]

Camden evidently considered the mound some kind of ancient territorial marker.

The main attraction dominating the mound's setting for much of the 20th century was the petrol station and cafe, present from the late 1920s, and although the subject of letters of protest from the archaeological community, it was extremely useful to local people. Gretchen Rawlins remembered with pleasure how the introduction of a jukebox in the cafe made it a hot spot for local teenagers.[7] Her sister-in-law, Marjorie, recalled climbing up the mound on

Sundays during the 1920s to watch the occasional car pass by and to observe a solar eclipse.[8] The mound also figured as an important backdrop to the lives of local people who fondly remember climbing it, rolling down it in the snow or doing their courting on it, and for many it formed a significant landmark. It had been so for generations. In the 18th century William Stukeley observed how 'The country people have an anniversary meeting at the top of Silbury-hill on every palm-Sunday, when they make merry with cakes, figs, sugar, and water fetch'd from the Swallow-head or spring of the Kennet'.[9] Such activities may have become quite widespread in Wiltshire at one time because similar events occurred at Cley Hill,[10] a natural Silbury Hill-like eminence near Warminster, and continued until the 1880s.[11] Evidently the tradition episodically survived through to the late 19th century at Silbury, for a letter to the *Salisbury Journal* in May 1892 refers to the tradition of eating figs on top of the mound.[12]

Refreshment rooms and petrol pumps to the west of Silbury Hill. The tea bungalow was present by 1928 when the first application for the siting of petrol pumps was made, and the photograph was probably taken in the 1930s. (AL0519/004/01/PA)

Similar festivities occurred at other times of the year. The *Bath Journal* for 7 September 1747 announced that

> At King Ceol's Theatre at Celbury-Hill [Silbury] near Marlborough (which is the most beautiful and magnificent mount in Europe) the 12th and 13th days of October, will be Bull-Baiting, Backsword Playing, Dancing, and other Divertions. The second day will be Wrestling, a Smock and Ribbons run for, and Foot-Ball Playing, eight of a Side. At this entertainment the Company of the Neighbouring Nobility, Members, Clergy, and the Rest of the King's Friends is desired; and as eleven years ago about Six Thousand People met at the said Hill, the Publick-Houses had not proper accommodation, therefore several Booths will be erected.[13]

A further traditional fair, usually held on the summit of Tan Hill, on the escarpment overlooking the Pewsey Vale, 3km to the south and prominently visible from Silbury, was held in the fields opposite the mound on August Bank Holiday on two occasions during the Second World War.[14]

In 1965, Gerald Hawkins published a popular account of his innovative interpretation of Stonehenge. Based on an early IBM computer analysis of the movement of certain celestial bodies, *Stonehenge Decoded* made a compelling case for the site being a complex calendrical device whereby one could use the sun's rays to predict certain solar events such as the midsummer solstice. At the height of the space race, the interpretation struck a chord with a generation seeking fresh meaning in a world that at any moment might face cold war calamity. With, on the one hand, the Beatles and others travelling to India to investigate eastern religion, and on the other, Dr Timothy Leary, the famous advocate of psychedelic drugs, encouraging youngsters to 'Turn on, tune in and drop out', the search for enlightenment took many forms.

Faced with Hawkins's ideas, Professor Richard Atkinson, excavator of Stonehenge and, during the 1960s, the voice of the archaeological establishment, could merely defend the archaeological status quo. Hawkins only applied his work to Stonehenge. The hundreds of other stone circles scattered across the

British countryside, for the moment, escaped the treatment. Consequently, outside the world of archaeology, the enormous monuments at Avebury avoided the notice of all but the most intrepid of tourists. While bringing the attention of thousands of television viewers to the area, even the presence of the BBC outside broadcast cameras recording the excavations of Professor Atkinson at Silbury Hill in 1968, 1969 and 1970 had little overall effect on visitor numbers. The rock festivals of the time had an altogether different result, especially that at Shepton Mallet in Somerset, when in 1970 thousands en route encountered the major prehistoric monuments of the West Country.

In 1974 the first rock festival was held at Stonehenge itself. Avebury escaped the vast numbers that annually descended on Stonehenge, but even among the alternative society there were small but significant numbers seeking other options. This was exacerbated when English Heritage decided to close Stonehenge to festival goers. Despite a small number of protesters at English Heritage's offices at Savile Row, the annual summer pilgrimage finished at Glastonbury, and while the Department of Health and Social Security office at Salisbury geared up with apprehension for the invasion of travellers, the village post office at Avebury generally welcomed the extra business. However, even small numbers swamped the village, and there was friction when some decided to pitch tents on private premises or when the post office was broken into. The zenith of these activities occurred during the late 1990s, principally focusing on the solar events of midsummer and midwinter, but interest has since waned and hardly a soul was present at the midwinter solstice in 2008.

The legacy, however, is a small but significant alternative religious community who visit for weddings and certain other ceremonies. Modern Druids, in particular, have established a presence and attempted to generate a connection with the land through a cycle of ceremonies around the various monuments, including offerings at Silbury Hill for a good harvest on 1 August. Very little is known of the original Iron Age Druids, and by the time they first appear in the record, Silbury Hill and the Avebury stone circles were over 1,500 years old and likely to have long lost their original significance. In contrast, the monuments that might well have played a central role in Iron Age ceremony, hillforts such as Oldbury to the west and Rybury to the south, both within 5km of Silbury, are completely ignored by modern Druids. Nevertheless, the latter have in the last decade become a familiar part of the landscape. Wiccans have also recently established a calendar of rituals based largely on respect for nature, and these events take place in harmony alongside the mainstream Anglican ceremonies.

Terry Dobney ('Terry the Druid') conducts a harvest festival on Silbury Hill on 1 August 2007. (661-7072-09)

In her book on Avebury village life between 1920 and 1974, Marjorie Rawlins[15] reflects on the changes and laments the loss of the self-sufficient community and its replacement with what is almost an archaeological theme park. Occasional tourists have always passed through, but the last two decades has seen an explosion in the numbers visiting. This attention is very much a product of modern society; of the global village. Various travel guides to Britain mention it and, like the Grand Canyon, the pyramids or Machu Piccu in other parts of the world, Avebury and Silbury have become one of the 'must see' sites of Britain, with the English Tourist Board channelling ever increasing numbers of visitors into the narrow lanes of Wiltshire. Coupled with an increasing popularity in Sunday pub lunches, at little more than an hour and a half's drive from London, the Avebury complex forms an attractive outing from the capital. By 1996 around half a million people each year visited the area.[16] Some have seen photographs or features on television and have an idea of what to expect, but for many this is their first encounter with prehistory, and they perambulate the stone circle and henge and stop in the lay-by at Silbury Hill and gaze in astonishment at the achievement of people who, 4,500 years ago, used stone, bone and wooden tools to construct this impressive structure. On first sight, others believe that Silbury Hill is a natural hillock or an overgrown industrial waste tip. After all, how on earth could such a mound be constructed without a mechanical excavator?

YEW

2 Kings, Druids and early investigations

Much of the country was looking forward to change. As in modern times, after a decade of any particular government the population becomes jaded and new directions are welcomed. Consequently, there was considerable optimism in 1660 about the political course that King Charles II would take following the restoration of the monarchy. Recrimination visited those who had been instrumental in introducing a republic, not least because of their role in bringing Charles I's rule to an abrupt end. A dozen of the protagonists were hanged, drawn and quartered, while members of a religious group who had tried to take over were similarly treated. Amongst supporters of the monarchy, however, there was a new confidence. Literature, both supportive and critical, flourished, while theatres, including the Theatre Royal at Drury Lane in London, were opened and encouraged by Charles who took an active role in their establishment.

Aubrey and the royal visit

Just a few months after the Restoration, the Royal Society of London for the Improvement of Natural Knowledge was formed, and one of its founding members, Walter Charleton, a physician and natural historian, investigated and reported on Stonehenge. He argued that in contrast to the view established by an earlier investigator, the prominent architect Inigo Jones, it was of Danish construction. John Aubrey, one of the Fellows of the Society, famous now for his potted, not to say refreshingly gossipy, biographies of prominent figures of the day, published as *Brief Lives*, was also familiar with Stonehenge. He was a

Wiltshireman who grew up at Easton Piercy near Leigh Delamere, the latter now changed beyond recognition by a service station on the M4 motorway, but his regular trips south across the downs to the family farm at Broad Chalke near Salisbury ensured his familiarity with the antiquity of that part of Wiltshire from an early age.

Dr Charleton and Viscount Brouncker, President of the Royal Society, had heard Aubrey claim that the great monument at Avebury 'did as much excel Stonehenge, as a Cathedral does a parish church', and during discussion about Stonehenge during 1663 conveyed this view to the king. Having met Aubrey the following day, King Charles asked to meet him two weeks later at Marlborough while the royal party was en route to Bath, evidently in order that he should receive a guided tour of the ancient monuments at Avebury. The king was so impressed that he instructed Aubrey to prepare a survey of the site; which he did in September of that year. The queen, however, perhaps less interested in the place, continued on her way, and Aubrey observed that 'As his Majesty departed from Avebury to overtake the Queen: he cast his eye on Silbury Hill about a mile off: which he had the curiosity to see, and walked up to the top of it, with the Duke of York. Mr Charleton and I attending them'.[1] The king was intrigued by some snails that lay about in good numbers on the summit, and Aubrey collected about a dozen for him. At Bath the following morning, while still in bed, the duke recalled the matter and mentioned it to the duchess, and asked Charleton to show her the snails. Whether this marked an interest in natural history or culinary expectation is not recorded. Nevertheless, the king's visit was undoubtedly a memorable occurrence for the villagers of Avebury and those in the locale of Silbury Hill, for it was still remembered by local people over 60 years later.[2]

Aubrey's plan of Avebury was a masterpiece. Like his assessment of Stonehenge, where his detailed observation recognised a circle of shallow depressions just within the bank, later referred to as the 'Aubrey Holes', his recognition of such detail was, for the time, exemplary. Using an elementary plane table,[3] he accurately surveyed the site and correctly depicted the earthworks of the surrounding banks and ditches as a series of straight lengths, where subsequent

John Aubrey, who escorted King Charles II and the Duke of York up Silbury Hill and made the first known illustration of the site; mezzotint, artist unknown. (© National Portrait Galley, London)

surveys inaccurately described it as a circle. Unfortunately Silbury did not command the same attention and later Aubrey lamented not having taken some basic measurements:

> I am sorry that I did not take the circumference at the bottom and top and the length of the hill, but I neglected it, because that Sir Jonas Moore, Surveyor of the Ordnance, had measured it accurately and also took the solid content [the volume], which he promised to give me, but upon his death, that (amongst many excellent papers of his) was lost.[4]

It was left to Sir Robert Moray, who had participated in the trip with King Charles, to provide a description:

> Selberry Hill is an Artificiall Mount or Tumulus standing in a Meadow higher & broader than the L[ord] Seamors [Seymours] mount yet flat at the top all over green, and of a steep ascent. It affordeth store of a sort of snail with a flat shell slender & having

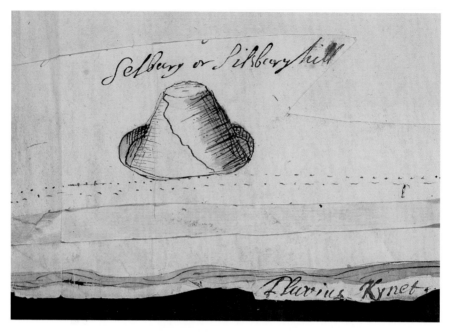

John Aubrey's sketch of Silbury Hill. (The Bodleian Libraries, University of Oxford. MS. Top. gen. c. 24, fol. 41v)

> 3 or 4 entire turns. There are in the subjacent meadow near the
> foot of the mount … vestiges of a Ditch out of which it seems the
> earth may have been taken to raise the mount … where usually in
> winter there stands some water.[5]

Aubrey did depict the mound in his general plan of Avebury, showing it in relationship to the other Avebury monuments, the stone circles, avenue and the Sanctuary. Although small, this is the first illustration of 'Selbury or Silbury hill', portraying a simple flat-topped conical mound, surrounded by a ditch and, importantly for archaeological interpretation, with a path to the summit in approximately the same position as the present one.[6] It is also thanks to Aubrey that we know something of the local traditions of Silbury Hill: 'No history gives us any account of this hill. The tradition that King Sil (or Zel as the country folk pronounce it) was buried here on horseback and that the hill was raised whilst a posnet of milk was seething'.[7] And again in a deleted sentence in his notebook: 'The country folk do call it Zelbury Hill and tell a story that it was raised over King Zel's grave'.[8]

The Druid and the drawings: Stukeley

Aubrey's work brought Silbury Hill to a wider audience, featuring as it did
in editions of the enormously popular *Camden's Britannia*, an enormous
accomplishment that described many of the known landmarks and historical
monuments around Britain. His own major work *Monumenta Britannica*
remained unpublished in his lifetime, and it was not long before it was
exceeded by that of William Stukeley, a Lincolnshire doctor turned clergyman.
Stukeley is arguably England's most famous antiquarian, with a particular
genius for drawing prehistoric landscapes. His drawings and engravings
combined artistic ability with a surveyor's accuracy, and for the first time
the complex of decaying monuments around Avebury and Silbury Hill was
provided with context and placed within their landscape setting. Not only
had he a superb eye for countryside and archaeological detail, but sketching,
depicting, and mapping such features was a considerable and difficult task.
It was a task that should not be underestimated, for he had to work out the
distances, curves, contours and lie of the land for himself, and the errors and
corrections are there for all to see in his manuscript drawings.

While generally remembered for his illustrations of the stone circles at
Stonehenge and Avebury, his greatest achievement was the depiction of these
monuments within their local environs, and his empathy with the chalk terrain is
quite evident. It may have been familiarity with similar subtly undulating chalk
hills and eroded coombes in his native Lincolnshire that inspired his intense
appreciation of the area, but he also brought with him the experience of having
visited and recorded many ancient monuments across Britain. Around Avebury,
the undulating downs, Cherhill Down, Waden Hill, Windmill Hill and other
prominent landforms were all depicted, while the position of the Kennet spring,
now known as Swallowhead spring, was recognised as of importance. This, he
noted, was once 'much more remarkable than at present, gushing out of the
earth, in a continued stream'.[9]

Stukeley spent a considerable amount of time in the Avebury area, particularly
in the summers of 1723 and 1724, and his observations remain of primary
importance. Benefiting from a fresh canvas and an enormous appetite for inquiry,

A portrait of William Stukeley; mezzotint by John Smith 1721.
(© National Portrait Galley, London)

he was able to observe, sketch and record features from a multitude of vantage points, as well as prepare plans of individual monuments. His panoramas demonstrated how the land was being utilised, depicting the hedged enclosures along the Kennet, and the extent to which the downs were being cultivated, but he also studied the archaeological sites in the wider chalk landscape of the Marlborough Downs: the prehistoric chambered tombs on Temple Downs, Clatford Bottom and Manton Field and elsewhere; Iron Age enclosures at Oldbury and Martinsell; and the motte of Marlborough Castle, then utilised as a garden mount. All were recorded in astute detail.

He visited Lord Hertford and his family at their house in Marlborough and prepared illustrations of the garden and Marlborough Mount, and he recorded how they returned the visit one day while he was working at Silbury. 'Lord Winchelsea, Lord Hertford, and the ladys came one day to visit the Druid as they called me; I treated them on the top of Silbury with a bowl of punch.'[10] He had clearly prepared for the visit, and his description suggests that he almost seems to have treated the summit of the mound as his studio. It was certainly a useful vantage point. From here he could see Avebury, little more than 1km to the north, and the earthworks on Windmill Hill beyond. The West Kennet long barrow lay to the south, and on the horizon Wansdyke and an array of round barrows and other monuments.

His illustrations entitled 'A view near the spot of the termination of Bekamton avenue July 19 1723', 'A prospect of Silbury hill from the Springhead of Kennet River 13 May 1724', 'Silbury Hill July 11 1723' and 'The Geometry of Silbury Hill' depict the mound as a simple truncated cone, often with little other detail, but variously with an indication of a terrace close to the top, and with the path in the position previously portrayed by Aubrey. Two ledges near the summit were depicted in one illustration as very slightly rising, while the summit was flat but just very slightly rounded. He observed that the mound was made of chalk, which he concluded had been obtained from the surrounding ditch.

William Stukeley's illustration 'Silbury Hill July 11 1723' showing Silbury as viewed from the main road and south-west of the Hill. (From Stukeley 1740–3)

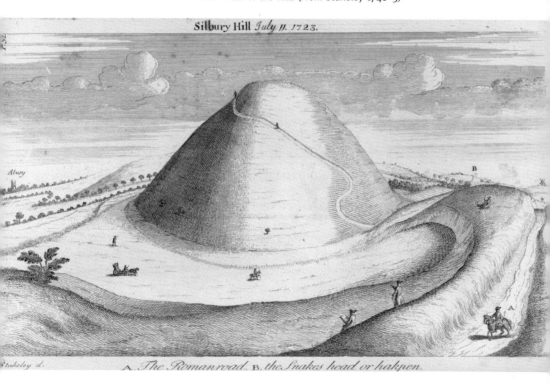

Basic, but nevertheless detailed measurements of the basal and summit diameters were provided and the volume calculated, and it was estimated that it would cost some £20,000 to construct in his day. He observed too that Silbury stood 'exactly south of Abury, and exactly between the extremities of the two avenues'. (It does not exactly – there is some 250m difference between Avebury and Silbury Hill.) He went on to describe the two causeways or isthmuses in the south, separated by a deep ditch, and believed these to have allowed access and passage to the summit for the large numbers of individuals involved in construction.

More importantly he described how in March 1723, Mr Holford, the lord of Avebury Manor, 'ordr'd some trees planted on this hill, in the middle of the noble plain or area at the top'. Presumably the lord of the manor aimed to use the mound as part of a designed landscape, an eye-catcher or mount, for Avebury Manor. Stukeley went on to record that 'the workmen dug up the body of the great king there buried in the centre, very little below the surface. The bones extremely rotten, so that they crumbled them in pieces with their fingers.'[11] During this work one of the workmen, John Fowler, recovered an iron chain or rather a solid mass of rust, which he later sold to Stukeley who tried some elementary conservation and immersed it in 'limner's drying oil' before drying it carefully. This seems to have worked well enough to allow it to be exhibited and drawn for illustration. Stukeley believed it to be part of the bridle or harness of a British king's chariot, and the surviving illustration of it does indeed show it to be a horse-bit, possibly of 11th-century AD date.[12] In addition, several antlers and an iron knife with a bone handle, all in a state of decay, were discovered from either the top or side of the Hill during these works.

To Stukeley, then, the burial was clearly that of the king for which the Hill had been raised, and the artefacts must have been grave goods. However, later in the 18th century, the Reverend James Douglas, an antiquarian and excavator of barrows, recorded that

> The bit of a bridle discovered by Stukeley, and his assertion of a
> monarch being buried there, has only the pleasure of conception
> to recommend it; it is not likely the monarch would have been
> buried near its surface, when such an immense mound of earth

had been raised for the purpose; and the time in raising it would not agree with the nature of a funeral obsequy, which must require a greater degree of expedition.[13]

Over a hundred years later, Charles Tucker, of the Royal Archaeological Institute, suggested that Stukeley may have been duped by 'the cunning John Fowler' and that the bridle may not have come from the Hill at all.[14]

There is, however, more to Stukeley's drawings than at first meets the eye. Heavily influenced by Aubrey's manuscript,[15] and following the historical orthodoxy of the time that before the Roman invasion the British Isles were led by Druids, he believed that the prehistoric monuments to be found in the countryside must be their temples. This was by no means a new idea, and while some people like Inigo Jones had elaborately argued that Stonehenge was definitely not Druidic in date (by which he meant pre-Roman), others considered that it was prehistoric, along with the Avebury monuments. Stukeley, however, took the idea further than any of his contemporaries. Combining classical and biblical sources, and mixing in a little mythology from around the world, he suggested that following the Great Flood, the Druids were the inheritors of the universal and true patriarchal religion of the Hebrews. The ancient religion of Druidism, he suggested, was the ancestor of Anglican Christianity and all the more pure because it was that much older.

Stukeley identified directly with this, taking on what was thought to be a Druidic-influenced name, 'Chyndonax', and he became affectionately known as 'the Druid' within his circle;[16] indeed, he had playfully been referred to as the Druid when visited at Silbury by Lord Hertford. His new interpretations of the Avebury complex embodied and reflected the presumed iconography of this ancient Druidic religion, which therefore became a representation of a circle (God's existence) being traversed by a serpent (God's creative power).[17] In this, Avebury formed the circle, the Beckhampton and West Kennet Avenues the serpent's body, and the stone and timber circle known as the Sanctuary was the head, all winding around Silbury Hill. (Stukeley deliberately elongated the Sanctuary monument in his later interpretations, so that it appeared more like a snake's head.)

Edward Drax with his wife Mary and their daughter Sarah. This was painted around the time that Drax was digging into Silbury. (Private collection. Courtesy of the Drax family. DP100306)

'All the wonderful remains of the old Patriarchal Religion'

There is no doubting Stukeley's contribution in providing surveys, illustrations and contemporary descriptions of the monuments and countryside, and with the publication of *Abury* in 1743 the fame of Avebury, Silbury Hill and the surrounding monuments was assured. Situated alongside the main road it is perhaps surprising that following the publication, Silbury did not immediately attract the attention of antiquarians keen to dig into it; perhaps it was its sheer volume that put them off. However, in 1776 Edward Drax, a colonel in the Dorset militia, proposed to do just that, and he decided that in the autumn he would dig a shaft from the summit down to the centre.

Drax held a number of estates in Wiltshire, at Etchilhampton, Bratton, and Coate, and at Bishops Cannings in the Vale of Pewsey, and would have been very familiar with the huge mound situated by the highway near Avebury.[18] He set up a subscription to fund the excavation and obtained the permission of the landowner, Arthur Jones. He was also intent on excavating one or two barrows that he saw as contemporary with Avebury and Silbury Hill. In June of 1776 he sought the financial co-operation of Sir John Pringle, the President of the Royal Society, on the basis that 'he [Drax] has some time had it in contemplation to search the contents of Silbury Hill, which has never been thoroughly examined into, and is perhaps one of the greatest monuments of antiquity in Europe'. Pringle believed that the request was more appropriate for consideration by the Society of Antiquaries of London and passed it to them, but they 'declined being any way concerned in the adventure'.[19] Drax then evidently turned to the Duke of Northumberland, Sir Hugh Smithson Percy. The duke had a reputation at court for an interest in science, and as a Trustee of the British Museum he was well versed in antiquarian pursuits and the provision of antiquities for

Hugh Percy, 1st Duke of Northumberland. Portrait by James Barry (1741–1806).
(The Bridgeman Art Library)

display. Perhaps also of some significance is that the duke was a coal-owner with experience of exploring geological strata for new seams and may have felt that he was able to provide knowledge and advice on methods of deep excavation. Along with subscribers from Bristol and Bath, appropriate funds were arranged.

On Saturday 2 November 1776, the *Bristol Journal* revealed that 'Silbury-Hill, the largest tumulus or artificial mound of earth in this kingdom, supposed to be of between 3 and 4000 years duration, was begun to be opened by the miners of Mendip, on Thursday last. They have made a hole at top of eight feet square. The Antiquarians promise to themselves wonders from the bowels of this mountain! It is situated between Devizes and Marlborough.' This account was repeated almost word for word in the *Salisbury and Winchester Journal* for Monday 4 November. None of these contemporary accounts mentions 'the Antiquarians' by name and the Salisbury version differs only in that it gives the date on which the excavations commenced as 'the 31st ult[imo]'. The 'correspondent' (perhaps Drax) would appear to have sent out what amounts to a press release. When set against the background of the developing events of the American War of Independence, antiquarian pursuits evidently appeared to some quite frivolous, and two weeks later, on Monday 18 November, a letter to the printer of the latter newspaper was published that mocked the purpose of the investigators. This was followed in turn on 2 December by a letter of support. Thereafter the columns fell silent.

Indeed, this investigation at Silbury was set against the backdrop of a series of important political and social events. Tensions with the settlers in North America had been increasing since 1773 when tea was thrown from the ships harboured at Boston, and warfare eventually commenced in 1775. Early in 1776 the English radical Thomas Paine anonymously published his pamphlet *Common Sense*, justifying the right of settlers in North America to self-determination. Then on 4 July the United States declared independence from the British Empire, and despite military successes on Valcour Island and Chatterton Hill towards the end of October, George III was forced to acknowledge that the war was not going as well as might be expected. The war took central stage in the concerns of politicians and general public alike, with stories of fifth columnists planning to set fire to ships at Bristol and Portsmouth bringing the war very much to the forefront of public awareness. At the very time the excavation was taking place at Silbury Hill, the country was on the alert for James Aitken, alias the notorious John the Painter. Later hanged for setting fire to shipyards in Portsmouth and Bristol, Aitken was caught in Hampshire in January 1777 after robbing a house in Calne, only 10km to the west of Silbury.

In 1793 the Reverend James Douglas described the excavations in his *Nenia Britannica*, naming those involved. He stated that

> The great hill of Silbury, generally considered as a barrow, was
> opened under the direction of the late Duke of Northumberland
> and Colonel Drax, under the supposition of its being a place of
> sepulture. Miners from Cornwall were employed, and great labour
> bestowed upon it. The only relic found at the bottom, and which
> Colonel Drax showed me, was a thin slip of oak wood: by burning
> the end of it in a wax taper, we proved it not to be whale-bone,
> which had been so reported; the smell of vegetable substance

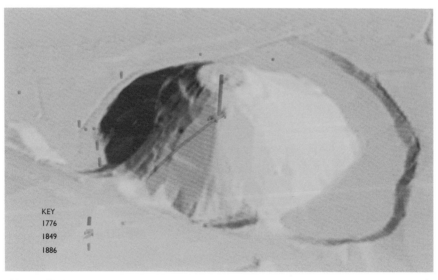

KEY
1776
1849
1886

Silbury Hill showing the locations of the 1776 shaft, the 1849 tunnel and some of the 1886 work.

soon convinced the Colonel of his mistake. He had a fancy that this hill was raised over a Druid oak, and he thought the remains of it were discovered in the excavation: there was, however, no reason for considering it to have been a place of sepulture by the digging into it.[20]

In his additions to *Camden's Britannia*, published a few years earlier, the antiquarian Richard Gough had more simply described the feature as 'a rotten post' and the only find a 'rusty knife'.[21]

Nothing else was known of the work at Silbury; a first-hand account was entirely missing. Colin Shrimpton, archivist at Alnwick Castle, kindly made a search but found no reference to the event amongst the Duke of Northumberland's archived material. Then, in 2008, two letters were unearthed in the British Library that had not been mentioned in any published account of the Hill and they were eagerly and minutely scrutinised with mounting excitement. The letters were written by Edward Drax while he was working on the site to a close family friend, George Pitt, Lord Rivers, who was the great-uncle of the famous archaeologist General Pitt Rivers.[22] Drax and Pitt had served in the militia together on the home front during the Seven Years War between 1756 and 1763 and had clearly established a good friendship, which comes through warmly in the letters. The first letter, dated 4 November 1776, describes the beginning of the excavation: the first six feet (1.8m) from the summit seems to have been disturbed ground, perhaps from the tree-digging episode that Stukeley had reported. They then reached the untouched deposits, and dug through chalk blocks 'the size of a man's head thrown in loosely'; at regular intervals they recovered fragments of deer antlers, discoveries that continued for 9.5m, the depth reached when the letter was written.

The second letter was written about a fortnight later by which time they were 95ft (29m) down and therefore very close to the bottom of the mound. By this point Drax and the miners had discovered 'a perpendicular cavity that as yet appears bottomless', which was some 150mm in diameter at the uppermost point. He went on to say that 'something that is now perished must have remained in this hole to have kept this cavity open, as the ground is loose chalk stones, and visibly nothing to support it'. Judging from this description the miners had stumbled across a void, which, as Drax suggests, may well have

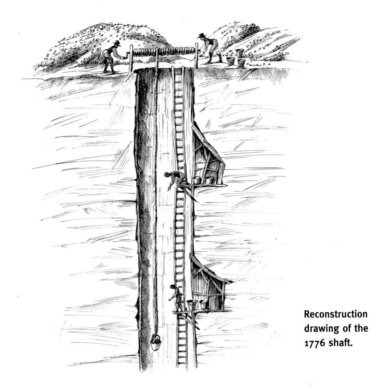

Reconstruction drawing of the 1776 shaft.

been the hole left by a timber post, long since rotted away. It seems then that we now have the origin of Drax's belief that the mound had been raised over a Druid oak. While this may be a fanciful interpretation, it does suggest that the early phases of the mound had perhaps been piled against a central post. He signed the last letter off saying that he waited 'with impatience the event of two or three days more as by that time we shall have come to where the stoppage is, and then I hope shall make a further Discovery'.

The letters make clear that he had a patriotic belief in the patriarchal Druidic origins for these monuments. His letters are suffused with Stukeley-esque language; he described how at Beckhampton he slept 'like an old Druid' (that is, like Stukeley) and 'contemplated all the wonderful remains of the old

Patriarchal Religion with which the environs of Abury abound', while even the 'sun shone on very luminously in the Patriarchal way'.

We do not know where the Silbury Hill artefacts are now; it seems from Douglas's account that Drax retained them. The precise motives of why Edward Drax chose to dig into Silbury Hill also remain uncertain. It is interesting to note that in the first of his letters he, not unexpectedly perhaps, related a comparison with the pyramids: 'I measured Silbury Hill as accurately as I could and am amazed at the ground that it stands upon[;] not much less than most of the Egyptian Pyramids except the great one which I think stands on near 11 acres.' This comparison was pointed out to illustrate more than size, and it is likely that both Drax and the Duke of Northumberland saw the mound in the same vein as the pyramids. James Bruce, a Member of the Royal Society who had travelled extensively in Egypt while searching for the source of the River Nile, studied many of the ancient monuments that he encountered at the tomb of Ramesses III in the Valley of the Kings in 1768. He visited London in 1774 with descriptions and marvellous illustrations of Egypt before returning home to Scotland and the subject will have been at the forefront of both popular and scientific discussion.

In 1773, the second volume of a new journal concerned with antiquities, *Archaeologia*, published by the Society of Antiquaries of London, contained an article about burial mounds on the Russian steppes, many of which, when opened, produced rich grave furnishings. Included was an illustration of the largest of these mounds, a barrow of Silbury-like proportions situated near Tomsky, which was opened by an officer and troops sent by the Russian court. The diggings found burials that were interpreted as those of a prince, his princess and his horse. Both human skeletons lay between sheets of gold; the male draped in a gold-bordered and jewel-bedecked cloth; the female similarly accompanied by gold and jewels.[23] The description is not so out of keeping perhaps with that of the burial of King Sil described by Aubrey years earlier. Just three years before the investigation of Silbury, the *Archaeologia* paper will almost certainly have come to the attention of Drax and the Duke and would no doubt have proved stimulating to potential subscribers.

Burial mound near Tomsky, Russia. Note the tree-lined path to the summit. (From *Archaeologia* 1773)

It may be the lack of fabulous finds or structures that inhibited publication, or perhaps it was fear of the mocking tone of the media, for further progress on digging the shaft was evidently not reported. For Drax, to announce evidence of a tree when so much more had been predicted would have been embarrassing. Meanwhile, the Duke of Northumberland's wife died in December 1776 and he was preoccupied in arranging an elaborate funeral for her in Westminster Abbey. [24] Both men, for their respective reasons, may have preferred to remain out of the limelight.

The excavation appears to have been completed by the end of the year and probably before the funeral, for early in the New Year a traveller passed by and observed that it was closed. This was Edward Williams, otherwise known as Iolo Morganwg, a stonemason and antiquary. Following the ideas of early antiquarians, he had pursued the idea of a modern Druidic institution, and indeed played a considerable role in establishing the British perception of them. On 12 January 1777 he passed through Beckhampton, en route from London to Wales, and observed that

> On my way hither I was so lucky as to be two days sick on the
> road. I suppose you would not be sorry to have as good an account

as I can give you of the opening of the Mountainous Tumulus at ABURY. I passed by it, and had the good fortune to meet with an intelligent shepherd, who saw it open (for it is now shut up) the gentleman who had it opened had the area of its base measured and found that it stood upon no less than eight acres of ground (which is but little less than that on which the largest of the Egyptian Pyramid stands) it is high in proportion and is never taken by the uninformed traveller but for a large natural mountain, there were four coal miners from Kingswood Coalmines near Bristol, employed for some Months to make a hole down to the bottom, they found it to consist of chalk and gravel thrown together by the hands of men and no natural hill as some doubted it to be, there were many cavities in it but for what purpose is unknown as nothing was found in them.[25]

Unlike Drax's letters to George Pitt and his press release announcing that the miners were from Mendip, or the later commentator, James Douglas, who indicated that they were from Cornwall, this letter suggests that the miners were from Bristol and actually names the colliery. The fact that the *Bristol Journal* was used to announce the excavation and that subscribers were obtained from the area shows that there may have been a strong Bristol connection. Situated to the east of Bristol, Kingswood Colliery, like Silbury, was on the London to Bristol road and relatively easy of access. Some of the Kingswood coal pits were of great depth and the 30 metres at Silbury would have been easily achieved. The Kingswood miners were said to be quite lawless, 'a wild race of colliers who … in the 18th century had struck terror into the law abiding hearts of the townsfolk of Bristol'. They often rebelled against pit owners and rioted within the city. On one occasion in 1709 some 400 of them 'armed with cudgels' entered the town to demand food. Later, following the protests of the agricultural community regarding the introduction of new toll roads in 1749, they needed little encouragement to join in and destroy the toll gates and houses, only to charge travellers for the privilege. For weeks they guarded Kingswood against the militia in order that ringleaders were not arrested. In the Bristol riots of 1831 their looting was said to be so extensive that they needed carts to take away the proceeds.[26]

In what state the miners left the Hill after they finished is unknown; miners traditionally left shafts open, though whether they made some attempt to backfill the shaft as part of Drax's deal with Arthur Jones, the landowner, is unclear. Like miners of this period, barrow diggers also rarely worried too much about the state of the monument after they had finished; the emphasis was generally on retrieving the objects inside. A search of the Bodleian Library at Oxford revealed two pen and ink wash illustrations made on 2 September 1788,[27] just 12 years after the shaft was sunk. They depict some scarring at the summit, but indicate that the Hill was recovering. Drax revealed in his letters that the miners had excavated a path, and these pictures illustrate some unusual lines of vegetation that could be the effect of access routes up the Hill. In particular, a ramp leading from the uppermost ledge almost to the summit is depicted in unusually sharp outline on the eastern slopes and could have played a role in the mining operations.

Pen and ink illustration of Silbury Hill from the west, 2 September 1788. One of a pair by an unknown artist (possibly Grimm, since a similar pair of illustrations in the British Library is signed Grimm, 1788) depicting the mound just 12 years after the work of Edward Drax. The milestone is in the same position today. (The Bodleian Libraries, University of Oxford. Gough Maps 33, fol. 10(a))

In 1849 the Very Reverend John Merewether, Dean of Hereford Cathedral, having lamented the lack of evidence about the 1776 excavation, said that mounds of spoil still survived which 'the excavators had not taken the trouble to throw in'.[28] An illustration drawn by William Lukis on 6 August 1849 after the visit to Silbury of the Archaeological Institute appears to depict a slump in the shaft about one-quarter the depth of the mound.[29] A little under 40 years later, Alfred Pass was altogether more charitable towards Drax, suggesting that 'all this material appears to have been refilled into the hole, excepting a small bank which is still visible on the flat summit'.[30]

Merewether went on to record the testimony of two local men. One was Richard Maskelyn, of Beckhampton, then aged 80, 'who had often heard his father tell of the miners out of Cornwall that cut into Silbury Hill; they went, as he heard, down to the bottom, and they found 'a man'.' The other was John Blake, of Avebury, then aged 95, who recalled that 'when the miners from Cornwall dug into Silbury Hill; it was when he was keeping company with his first wife, and was about twenty years of age. He went with her to see the place, and they cut her gown. They went down to the bottom, and found a man.' These accounts could be alluding to human remains being found at the base of the shaft; however, this does not fit with the account presented by Douglas in 1793, and it could be that the miners were playing tricks on them. Certainly Merewether adjudged that these two old men were 'led to infer what was expected'.[31]

The Royal Archaeological Institute and the 1849 tunnel

Following Drax's intervention, the mound lay undisturbed for 73 years, then increasing interest coupled with appropriate opportunity resulted in a further bout of investigation. The Age of Steam introduced a transport revolution allowing greater movement around the country. By 1841 the construction of the Box Tunnel made it possible to travel from London to Bristol by courtesy of Isambard Kingdom Brunel and the Great Western Railway. Having decided upon Salisbury in Wiltshire as the venue for its annual meeting, the Central Committee of the recently formed Royal Archaeological Institute arranged for an investigation into the mound to take place that summer, which was later stated as being in response to the requests of interested members.

The committee sanctioned Richard Falkner, a banker from Devizes, and Henry Blandford, a civil engineer from Rowde who was experienced in the construction of cuttings and embankments for railways, to undertake a preliminary investigation; this involved digging some exploratory trenches to determine the position of the old land surface, as well as the preparation of a plan. The location of these trenches is not known, but the resulting plan[32] depicts the base of the mound as a dashed line, together with the position of

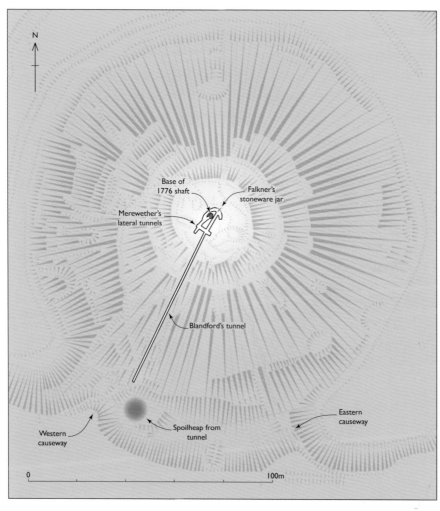

The position of the tunnel excavated by Henry Blandford for the Archaelogical Institute in 1849, set against a more recent survey of the surface earthworks whereby the hachures represent slopes. Merewether's lateral tunnels and other explorations lie at the centre of the mound.

the ditch in the east and the base of the quarry extension on the west. Having concluded their work, the pair made recommendations about the best location from which to drive a tunnel to the centre of the mound, and they were subsequently asked to carry out the work; a budget of £30 was agreed to allow for labour, equipment and backfilling.

Turf was stripped on the 9 July, and excavation of the tunnel followed. At 2m high and just short of 1m wide – enough to allow passage of a navvy with laden wheelbarrow – it was dug along the old land surface towards the centre of the mound. Although it was very narrow, gangs of workmen were employed and a shift system operated, so that work was carried on around the clock. The tunnel was started from the westernmost of two causeways across the ditch situated to the south of the mound. Starting below ground level in the chalk bedrock, the tunnel inclined upwards and finally broke through into the old land surface at a distance of around 30m from the entrance. Here the mound was composed of 'brownish earth chalky rubble',[33] and that level was subsequently followed towards the centre of the mound. From this point in the tunnel it was necessary to use props to support the roof. By the date of the annual meeting they had reached the estimated centre at a distance of 49m. By the time the members of the Institute had visited the site on 31 July and 1 August, the tunnel had gone

beyond the centre of the mound. At the very centre it was discovered that 'sods of turf and moss in layers appeared to be of the greatest thickness … curving layers of turf lying one over the other … The turf was quite black, as was also the undecayed moss and grass which formed the surface of each layer, and amongst it were the dead shells *etc*.'[34]

By now the budget was exhausted, but the opinion that further explorations should be made resulted in a group of members, led by Merewether and including the Reverend John Bathurst Deane (the future grandfather of the author P G Wodehouse), making an appeal for supplementary funding. By the end of the week most members and observers had left, though the Reverend Merewether, who had visited the excavations en route to the meeting and taken a room at the Waggon and Horses at Beckhampton, remained to observe progress and instructed that lateral excavations should be made to both east and west. A number of silicified sandstone boulders known as sarsen stones were encountered in one of the lateral excavations on the east side, and 'they were much worn and similar to those found in the surrounding fields',[35] Merewether reported that they were

> placed with their concave surface downwards, favouring the line of the heap … as is frequently seen in small barrows and casing as it were the mound. On the top of some of these were observed fragments of bone, and small sticks, as of bushes … and two or three pieces of the ribs of either the ox or red deer … also the tine of a stags antler.[36]

Merewether also noted that there were 'great quantities of moss still in a state of comparative freshness'[37] and that it still retained its colour. He believed that this material, together with the freshwater shells, had come from a moist location and thought that it must have derived from the west, north or east sides of the Hill where the Beckhampton Brook flowed past the foot of the mound. Sealing the turf stack was a dense black layer of organic material containing fragments of small branches and emitting a peculiar smell. In addition, fragments of what he thought were plaited grass or string were discovered in this organic deposit. This was not recorded in any of the later excavations and is likely to have been fungal mycelium, probably introduced in 1776.

John Merewether, Dean of Hereford, a native of Wiltshire who attended the meeting of the Archaeological Institute in Salisbury in 1849 and used the visit to dig into 35 barrows on the downs around Avebury as well as assume control of the Silbury Hill excavations for a period, all in four weeks.
(© The Trustees of the British Museum)

On Monday 6 August Falkner and Blandford, perhaps fed up with the interferences of Merewether, considered the task completed according to the agreement with the Royal Archaeological Institute. Merewether, however, remained driven and, clearly convinced that the chances of possible discoveries had not been exhausted, informed the Institute that he would take over: 'and it was arranged that I should be left in charge'.[38] He subsequently asked the workmen to cut a diagonal tunnel, which encountered the base of the shaft sunk by the miners in 1776, and then a curving tunnel northwards following the line of the central mound. Perhaps because little evidence of burial or artefacts was forthcoming, he abandoned the site almost immediately and returned to his investigation of local barrows. Finally, on 15 August 1849, Merewether left Wiltshire, but the excavations at Silbury Hill continued until the end of the month, this time directed by the Reverend John Bathurst Deane.

Roof props from the central area that could be withdrawn in safety were recovered, but the project had been overextended by enthusiastic antiquarians, and resources were exhausted. Backfilling of the tunnel was not carried out, and the extracted chalk was left in the ditch outside the tunnel entrance. The tunnel was finally closed up in September, being sealed with a brick wall a little within the entrance and covered over. Just before this, Falkner deposited two stoneware jars, one in the middle of the tunnel and one by the entrance, as time capsules. The jar in the middle (the only one to have been retrieved) contained 21 items, including coins, a lead plaque, pamphlets, a newspaper and a poem by Emmeline Fisher,[39] who was a second cousin to William Wordsworth. The official account of the excavation was written up for the Committee of the Royal Archaeological Institute by Charles Tucker, to which the memoirs of Merewether, who died soon afterwards, add interesting detail and colour, but unfortunately we know nothing of the work led by Bathurst Deane, and the search for an account continues.

The dark streak representing the old ground surface was unbroken wherever it was investigated and there was consequently no evidence for a central grave. The only finds were some fragments of antler and a few animal bones, evidently from the mound matrix. Charles Tucker commented that they 'may have been thrown up with the earth from the meadow below when the hill was formed'. For Tucker, the excavations had disproved the idea that a burial lay at the centre. They disproved, too, the idea that that the mound lay over the Roman road. Instead, as Stukeley had earlier observed, the road took care to avoid the mound, which was therefore of earlier date than the Roman period.[40]

The Roman road and differences of opinion

A decade after the Institute had dug their tunnel into the centre of the mound, James Fergusson, a prominent writer on architecture and antiquarian matters, attempted to demonstrate that the mound was built later than the Roman road.[41] Fergusson believed that the position of the various monuments and stones around Avebury were set in position to commemorate King Arthur's victory at the battle of Mount Badon. The lines of stones represented soldiers and, like the mound at Waterloo, in Belgium, Silbury Hill had been constructed to commemorate the event. Sir John Lubbock along with others disputed this, but a key part of Fergusson's thesis lay in the fact that he considered Silbury to have been constructed over the road. Local Wiltshire archaeologists, such as the Reverend Alfred Charles Smith, believed they knew exactly where the course of the road was: in the field to the south. Although cultivated it was still possible to see it as an earthwork. Indeed, Stukeley had illustrated and commented upon it so many years before. Nevertheless, the challenge was taken up by the newly founded Wiltshire Archaeological and Natural History Society (WANHS).

Along with Fergusson, members of the society discussed where to place trenches, and in 1867 two were excavated on the east side of the mound at the estimated original ground level. One trench was dug either side of where the road was expected to be, although the size and precise location of each trench are now unclear. The northernmost, however, revealed a series of chalk blocks, each about 300mm (12 inches) in diameter, located just below the turf, and at just over 500mm (18 inches) deep six fragments of red deer antler were recovered.[42] The southern trench was sited 'by a depression which reaches nearly one third of the way up the hill and would seem to have been caused by some disturbance at the foot', and this revealed 'a distinct semicircular space about 10 feet in radius' that had been 'hollowed out. The surface was irregular, and on a ledge about eighteen inches higher than the rest, three feet square, and four feet within the hill, there was a deposit of wood ashes, in the middle of which, and lying side by side, were the blade of an iron clasp knife … and a small whetstone'.[43] Strangely, the old ground surface was not encountered, and the Reverend Prebendary John Wilkinson suggested that it had been deturfed to provide material for the core of the mound.[44] Unfortunately for Fergusson, no trace of the road was found.

Attention then turned to the field to the south where the earthwork remains of the road were encountered. Nine sections were cut across it, enough to demonstrate that it curved to avoid the southern lip of the mound's ditch. As they tried to trace its course across the lower ground and up the other side, they commented on the presence of a large number of coins and surface undulations that appeared to mark the site of a building.[45]

'A rude race of hunters': Alfred Pass and the ditch

Twenty years later attention turned for the first time to the massive ditch encircling Silbury Hill, as well as its extension in the west. In 1886 a series of small excavation trenches were cut in the meadow at the base of the Hill by Alfred Pass, a member of a British archaeological society, and the location of each was depicted on a plan prepared by the Bristol surveyors Ashmead and Son. They were described as shafts and were situated on the ditch floor to the west and north of the mound. The size of each of these is unknown, but workmen digging them were described in the plural, so that each hole must have been large enough to take at least two individuals. In each case the shaft was taken down to the natural solid chalk, mostly to a depth of some 4.5m, but around the foot of the mound the depth increased to about 6.5m below the surface.[46]

Few finds were encountered, though some flint flakes and bones were noted from one of the shafts. In another, at about 3m from the surface, the clay appeared to have been stained almost black for about 300mm. At this level a human femur was discovered and beneath this lay a further 1.5-metre deposit of unstained clay. Alfred Pass retained the soil and washed it through a sieve, and a number of flint flakes were uncovered.[47] The presence of flint artefacts led him to suggest that Silbury 'was erected by a people, probably a rude race of hunters, so little advanced in civilisation, that they were using flint implements a long time after the hill was built'.[48] Animal bones of deer, ox, pig, and dog were also recovered; indeed, remnants of deer and ox bones were found in all but one shaft, sometimes associated with small burnt sarsen stones.[49] In one shaft, situated close to the base of the mound and ditch terminal, a coin of Marcus Aurelius was retrieved from a depth of nearly 2m, indicating perhaps that the upper third of the ditch deposits had accumulated since the Roman period. The general view was that the site was sepulchral or ritual in nature, but given this interpretation, what such a massive ditch represented was neatly ignored.

Sir John Lubbock saves Silbury for the nation

By the time Alfred Pass's work was underway, one of the most influential figures of the Victorian antiquarian scene had already entered the stage: Sir John Lubbock, a wealthy banker with a keen interest in prehistory. Lubbock was

John Lubbock

Sir John Lubbock, the first Lord Avebury, who purchased Silbury Hill and placed it within the guardianship of the state; collotype 1896. (© National Portrait Gallery, London)

also a political man, and played a significant role in providing legal protection for ancient monuments (another of his great political achievements was the introduction of bank holidays). He published *Pre-Historic Times* in 1865, a hugely influential book that has been described as 'the archaeological equivalent of Darwin's *On the Origin of Species*'.[50] Indeed, Charles Darwin and Lubbock were friends and neighbours.

John Lubbock was familiar with Silbury Hill, having dug there with Wilkinson in 1867, and so when the estate around Silbury was put up for auction in 1873, Lubbock, then the Wiltshire Archaeological and Natural History Society's President, and acting on information supplied by the vicar of Avebury, the Reverend Bryan King, persuaded the landowners 'to apportion Silbury and a small plot immediately around it as a separate lot'.[51] He purchased this lot himself and placed it within the guardianship of the then recently created Ancient Monuments Board; Silbury Hill was thus generously preserved for the nation. In 1900 Lubbock was awarded a peerage for his political work and chose the title Lord Avebury – a testimony to his love of the archaeology of the area.

Blackthorn

3 Into the 20th century: Petrie, Atkinson and the BBC

'Sir, I have the honour to inform you that the chalk has fallen in on the side of Silbury Hill', wrote the Deputy Constable of Wiltshire to the Secretary of the Ministry of Works on 24 March 1915, '… exposing a tunnel, no doubt an ancient excavation. The entrance is very small but people can get in and it is quite possible an accident may happen'. The tunnel excavated by the Archaeological Institute appears to have fallen in noticeably during the First World War, at least by the entrance. One reliable authority, H C Brentnall, a local archaeologist and historian based at Marlborough College, wrote in 1949 to R S Newall, curator of Salisbury Museum, recalling that 'In 1915 I crawled to the centre of Silbury along the 1849 gallery. There were sarsens suspended over my head at the end of the gallery in the centre. If they were to be attributed to a chamber I must have entered by the cellar.'[1]

Mrs L F Brooks of 22 Stratton Road, Pewsey, was quoted in the *Marlborough Times* in August 1962 as describing how during the First World War she used to live very near the hill and was told by her parents that there were caverns inside. When the entrance caved in, in 1915, a tiny passage led first of all downwards and then altered course and proceeded upwards. Eventually it forked, with one way leading to a dead end and the other to a cavern 'about as big as a room'. Beyond this there was another cavern similar to the first: 'We took candles in with us and used to write our names on the ceiling with the candle smoke'. She described the passages as very small: 'We had to crawl, a grown up couldn't have

Photograph, probably taken in 1922, showing the position of a new notice and the door blocking the collapsed tunnel. (AL0519/005/02/PA)

got through. The whole system must have gone about three parts through the hill,' she said. 'And it was very frightening … my brother would blow out the candle and I would be terrified.'[2]

Members of the Royal Archaeological Institute and the Wiltshire Archaeological and Natural History Society visiting in 1920 observed that 'the blocking of the entrance has fallen, so that anyone who likes to take the risk can crawl in and see whatever is to be seen'. Eventually the entrance was sealed up with a wooden door, but when that proved ineffective at stopping people getting in, a steel door was permanently erected in its place – having returned to England from active service in the First World War, local archaeologist Arthur Passmore had convinced the archaeological society to fit this new steel door, and it was covered over in May 1923.[3]

Petrie at Silbury

Flinders Petrie, the famous Egyptologist, had surveyed archaeological field monuments in Kent and Wiltshire, including Stonehenge. Temporarily in Britain, he now turned his attention to the mound. Perhaps he saw Silbury as a British pyramid, or maybe he was just looking for a high-profile excavation to rival Stonehenge. He produced a measured profile that most interestingly indicates that the position of the 1776 shaft on the summit was still visible; indeed, an air photograph taken in 1925 indicates that it was open at this time. He made no comment on this, but instead focused his attention on the eastern 'neck' or causeway and determined that it was of solid chalk, the outer slope of which had been covered with chalk rubble in order to 'form a smooth gradient from the road down to the neck'.[4]

Sir Flinders Petrie, field archaeologist and prominent Egyptologist; half-plate glass negative by Walter Stoneman, 1917. (© National Portrait Gallery, London)

During the later part of August 1922, Petrie excavated two small parallel trenches on the lower slope of the mound opposite the eastern causeway, which were intended to intercept any entrance into the mound that lay along the line of the 'neck'. As Wilkinson and the others from the WANHS had discovered previously, the turf of the original land surface here appeared to be absent, leading Petrie to consider that the ground level had been cut into or lowered.

Petrie did, however, rediscover seven of the eight sarsens that Merewether had previously noted as being located around the base of the mound, but indicated that they were not as precisely positioned as Merewether had indicated. He gave measurements to them from a fencepost and also mentioned that about 30 sarsens had been reused in recent times to support carts across the ditch,[5] although exactly where or why was not recorded. Assuming similar intervals around the base, Petrie indicated that if the stones formed a circle there would have been originally 250 stones – each just over 2m apart. Few sarsens remain today. There are several on the outer slope of the ditch on the eastern side of the mound, while others have been broken up and lie sparsely scattered along the course of the stream bed. It is quite conceivable, however, that the area was once covered with such naturally occurring stones, as many parts of the Marlborough Downs were until recently.

As there was access, Petrie was able to investigate the 1849 tunnel and inspect the deposits exposed in the tunnel walls. He determined that the mound chiefly consisted of deposits of chalk rubble and yellow clay, usually laid horizontally. Many fragments of antler, bones of red deer and pig, and flint flakes were recovered from his excavations on the south-eastern slope, mostly at a depth of between 2.5m and 3m. Amongst his conclusions, encouraged by Passmore's similar deduction which he had published two years previously, and presumably interpreting Richard Gough's 1789 addition to *Camden's Britannia*, Petrie mentioned a central tree that was thought to have been found when digging the shaft in 1776, and he speculated that a cord stretched horizontally from such a feature would allow level construction work to take place.[6] Knighted in 1923 for services to Egyptology and British archaeology, Petrie soon left Silbury Hill behind him and headed for Palestine.

The BBC prepares to dig

Silbury took a back seat between the two world wars and during the 1950s, as nearby monuments Windmill Hill, Avebury, the West Kennet stone avenue and West Kennet long barrow were excavated. Attention had also focused on Stonehenge, in particular a major intervention by Professor Richard Atkinson, then of Edinburgh University. Atkinson was one of the best-known archaeologists of the day, conducting a series of high-profile excavations – his book, based on these excavations, remained the standard account of Stonehenge's history and phasing until the mid-1990s. As part of the excavations, a TV programme had been arranged by Paul Johnstone for the BBC, marking a further link between television and archaeology. The consumer boom of the late 1950s and early 1960s saw television sets installed in almost every household, and millions of people glued to the set each night eagerly devoured everything that was presented. People often watched until the National Anthem announced close-down and the test card sent the nation to bed. According to Atkinson, it was John Irving of the BBC in Bristol who in 1960 first suggested a sponsored excavation at Silbury.[7] At that time, though, Atkinson's mind was still on Stonehenge, and along with his colleague Stuart Piggott, tried to re-focus the BBC funding into the excavation of a series of long and round barrows within the immediate vicinity. In the event the money offered was insufficient, and the project was dropped.

From the early 1950s the television quiz show *Animal, Vegetable, Mineral?* did much to introduce the public to archaeology. In this programme a panel of archaeologists including Mortimer Wheeler and Glyn Daniel (who, in 1954 and 1955 respectively, were voted TV personality of the year for their role), knowledgeably pronounced upon ancient artefacts placed in front of them. However, attitudes in Britain were changing rapidly, and by the middle of the decade this format had become decidedly stuffy. On its heels came *Buried Treasure*, and this was followed in the mid-1960s by *Chronicle*, a monthly programme presented by Magnús Magnússon, which was to cover all manner of current archaeological projects and excavations at home and abroad. Advances in technology allowed for much greater flexibility, and programmes could be broadcast from outside, capturing the immediacy of archaeological excavations.

David Attenborough, the controller of BBC2 (who had previously worked on *Animal, Vegetable, Mineral?* and had commissioned *Chronicle*), Desmond Hawkins, the head of the BBC West region; and Paul Johnstone and David Collison of *Chronicle*, approached Atkinson, who was now based at Cardiff University, for a second time with an idea to open a tunnel into the heart of Silbury.[8]

It may have been the work of F R McKim several years earlier that influenced Atkinson. Advances in technology were beginning to find applications in archaeology, and during the late 1950s McKim had made an attempt to locate a burial chamber in Silbury Hill by using electrical resistivity methods. Unlike previous investigators he considered that any burial might lay off-centre and may have remained undetected by either shaft or tunnel.[9] A series of probes were placed in the ground, and an electrical current was sent between them and the resistance levels recorded. It was considered that buried features would appear as areas of greater or lesser resistance than the norm. Resistivity readings were taken around part of the base and another at approximately half-way up the mound. The process is now well established in archaeology, but for the time was groundbreaking. The technique was innovative and exploratory, although unfortunately on this occasion the results proved unsatisfactory and inconclusive. However, the possibility of using such original and pioneering methods appears to have appealed to Atkinson and, at the peak of his career and with the excavations at Stonehenge behind him, he agreed to the proposal.

Preparations continued slowly through the hot summer of 1966, and by 1967 a project outline had been prepared that carefully assessed gaps in knowledge about the mound and how they might be addressed.[10] The project was certainly ambitious. Atkinson re-emphasised that this was 'the largest artificial mound in Europe … substantially larger than the smallest of the three pyramids at Gizeh in Egypt' and reiterated the tradition that a horse and rider 'the size of life, and of solid gold' was buried within.[11] Atkinson, of course, would not have taken this literally, but following earlier writers he did consider that on balance 'the most likely hypothesis is that it is a burial mound of exceptional size'.[12] Indeed, as early as 1956 he had suggested that a burial lay beneath Silbury Hill: 'Yet who but he should sleep, like Arthur or Barbarossa, in the quiet darkness of a sarsen vault beneath the mountainous pile of Silbury Hill? And is Stonehenge itself his memorial?'[13] Film makers had previously picked up on this, and in 1964 *The Mystery of Stonehenge* made for CBS news by Harry Morgen, Atkinson suggested that Silbury Hill was where the 'great chief' who built Stonehenge was buried. Atkinson's outline explained the reason for the excavation to the general public. The prospect of discovering an interesting and rich burial must have heartened the BBC. Both they and the archaeological community were fully signed up to the prospect of great discoveries.

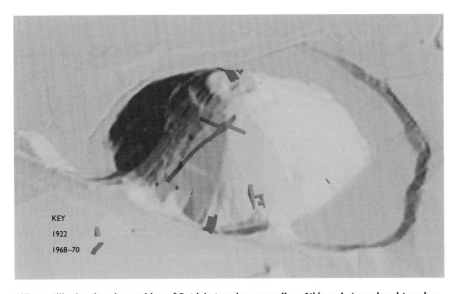

KEY
1922
1968–70

Silbury Hill, showing the position of Petrie's trenches as well as Atkinson's tunnel and trenches.

The easiest method of accessing the interior was by way of the tunnel created in 1849. After all, Petrie and others had entered it earlier in the century, and despite roof falls it was a convenient way of getting to the centre. It was also the most economical, and in addition had merit in that it avoided causing further damage to the Hill. Atkinson canvassed for the eyewitness accounts of others who may have seen or entered the tunnel while it was accessible during the First World War. Amazingly, he received 35 responses,[14] a dozen of which referred to a chamber in the central area. 'I think that the central cavern was some 20–25ft [6–7.6m] in diameter, that there were six or eight holes or passages leading off.'

Another said that a 'slightly sloping terminal opened into chambers at intervals', and yet another wrote that 'there were seven small tunnels which all led into a small chamber'. Some referred to a fork in the passage: 'whichever way you go you complete a circuit and come back on yourself'. This presumably referred to the circuitous tunnel cut by Merewether. One suggested that one of the side passages had been blocked, 'but the dead end was wide and higher with a brick wall on the left side'. Two, in rather vague fashion, mentioned surviving timbers, although six others indicated that no timbers were to be seen, from which it was possible for Atkinson to conclude that 'little if any of the original timbering was left in position in 1849'. One correspondent wrote that 'It was very dry … there were no timbers supporting the roof', while others contradicted this and said that it was very damp.

Members of the Royal Flying Corps (later Royal Air Force) based at nearby Yatesbury would regularly take a breather and shelter from rain at Silbury while on their cross-country runs. Mony Page, from Christchurch in Hampshire, said that 'in 1917 while serving with the Royal Flying Corps at Yatesbury I crawled into the tunnel out of curiosity. I did not venture very far having no torch and I remember being a bit scared too', while G Holt from Worthing wrote that 'In 1918 I was in the RAF stationed at Yatesbury, quite close to Silbury Hill and in those days (more than 50 years ago) an exploratory tunnel had already been dug right through the hill, and I have actually been through from one side of the hill to the other, crawling on hands and knees.' Presumably he had gone around the circuitous tunnel and exited via the entrance. There are hints from this of a number of roof falls, both at the entrance and further inside, but the descriptions appear to indicate that beyond the entrance, the tunnel first opened in 1849 was still open and accessible.

Atkinson was also concerned to investigate the external structure of the mound. Preliminary visits allowed him to observe that a marked terrace or step occurred on the upper slopes, with apparent traces of others lower down: 'These suggest that the mound was perhaps constructed originally in the form of a stepped cone, and that most of the steps, particularly towards the bottom, have been obliterated by subsequent weathering.' He noted that the trenches cut by Petrie in 1922 suggested that the main mound was 'built up in horizontal layers' and considered that excavation trenches placed on the summit and upper slopes could illuminate these points.[15] Besides the few small shafts dug by Alfred Pass in 1886, very little work had been carried out on the ditch, yet it might be expected to act as a superb receptacle for artefacts. If below the water table, organic material might also survive. There was some caution and doubt regarding the structural interpretation, or even the existence, of the sarsens that were said to lie around the base of the mound, and these would be investigated and examined. Finally, Atkinson returned to the question of the Roman road. Despite the work of A C Smith and others during the 19th century, no plan of the excavations of the Roman road seemed to exist, so a programme of geophysical survey and excavation was planned to confirm its course.

Consequently, an ambitious campaign was devised that would last three summer seasons, the first involving various surveys, while the latter two, to be supported by the BBC, proposed excavations in five areas. Assistance for other non-invasive work was sought from elsewhere. In 1967 the Geography Department of Bristol University would establish a site grid and prepare a contour survey of the site, while the Zoology Department at Southampton University would study the modern fauna. The Nature Conservancy Council, who considered the vegetation of importance and who wished to schedule the area as a Site of Special Scientific Interest, would carry out a similar survey of the flora.[16] The following year geophysicists from the Geology Department at Cardiff University would make borings through the mound and ditch to establish their composition and determine whether the mound structure was consistent or whether anomalies existed. Echo-detecting equipment would also be brought in to discover the depth and form of the bottom of the ditch. The focal point that year, however, would be the re-opening of the 1849 tunnel. During the third season, in July–August 1969, the excavations at the centre would be completed, while further trenches would be placed on the summit, slopes and in the ditch. Accordingly, the scene was set for one of the most extraordinary of modern archaeological interventions.

Atkinson goes in

Work began in 1967 during the Summer of Love with, ironically, the Vietnam War raging. Atkinson was keen to have an accurate plan of the mound that depicted the ledges that he knew were present on the slopes so that he could accurately place trenches across them. The survey resulted in a plot of the mound, with contours spaced at 2m intervals – the best yet. Unfortunately, however, this was too coarse an interval to depict the slight earthworks and undulations that Atkinson knew were present on the slopes. The problem was solved by experimenting with an innovative approach. Mapping of features on the ground by plotting from air photographs viewed stereoscopically had been done before, but the technique had developed enormously during the Second World War and Cold War years. John Hampton of the National Monuments Record was pioneering the method in archaeology and arranged for a series of overlapping vertical photographs to be taken from the air. The result was a plan of contours at 500mm intervals that provided at least some indication of the terraces and surface undulations and allowed the trenches to be positioned in relation to the site grid.

Late that summer, following changes at the BBC that reflected the public mood, the first *Chronicle* programme on BBC television was broadcast. On the radio the BBC Light Programme was abandoned and Radio 1, which employed the DJs from former pirate radio stations Caroline, London and others broadcasting from the Thames Estuary, was established. On television, BBC2 had been running programmes since 1964. Now the excavation of Silbury Hill in September 1967 demanded a new approach. It was televised live using the outside broadcast team.

Early in 1968 the infrastructure was set in place: fencing, site huts, a platform in front of the tunnel entrance, a bridge of scaffolding across the ditch, caravans, telephone lines, and a water supply for archaeological purposes, cooking and to provide hot showers for those working underground. All was ready for an initial two-week period of excavation in April, during which a new tunnel was bored in order to obtain access to the old one. In view of the roof falls at the entrance to the 1849 tunnel it was thought safer to create a new entrance. This

Some of the site infrastructure for the 1968 work. A latrine tent can be seen in the foreground.
(From the Alexander Keiller Museum archive)

was slightly above and east of the old one and was designed to intersect the 1849 tunnel at about 20m into the interior of the mound when the obstructions were cleared. That April was particularly cold, and Atkinson recalled how the frosty weather had frozen the water supply and prevented the showers from working.[17] However, the work still went ahead.

The surveys of various kinds continued, with the aim of obtaining a vertical section through both mound and ditch. A drilling rig was set up on the summit of the mound to drill a series of boreholes down through it to the former ground surface, while a series of cores were drilled down the south-west slope of the mound. This was an astonishing archaeological operation and provided a superb insight into the structure of the mound. To the north of the mound a hammer seismograph was used to profile the ditch and this was augmented by borings which provided material for environmental analysis. The responses indicated that the ditch was over 5m deep immediately adjacent to the fence around the base of the mound, then it sloped down to a maximum of just over 9m deep at 27m north of the fence before rising rapidly. A step 500mm deep occurred at 18m from the fence. The auger holes through the deposits revealed that the silts comprised some 3m of grey silty clay overlying chalk and flint gravel. Barbara Hart-Jones, who studied the deposits, considered that as the snail shells recovered were water snails the ditch must have been water filled. Atkinson, however, believed that the ditch could not have been dug if the ground was wet and so postulated that a stream had entered the ditch and deposited its silt during the Bronze Age. When the drill rigs were clear of the summit a geophysical survey was carried out, but the results were unfortunately confused by the presence of chicken wire that had been laid over the surface as a conservation aid a few years earlier and interfered with the readings.

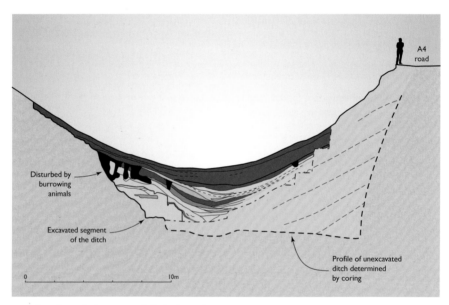

A section through the external ditch. (Based on Atkinson's excavation and after Whittle 1997)

Alongside this, work began on the tunnel and the outside broadcast unit moved in. Hopes were high, since a spearhead (thought to be of Saxon origin) was recovered whilst erecting a post in advance of an official launch to the excavations. The *Birmingham Evening Mail* of 8 April 1968 reported that the first find at the 'mystery mound' had been made even before excavations had begun. Atkinson later recalled how the difficult task of tunnelling was carried out by staff and students of the Mining Department at Cardiff University, under the watchful eye of Dr John Taylor and a retired South Wales coal miner, Bill Curtis. The latter constructed a concrete portal for the entrance complete with the date '1968' embossed on it (which, Atkinson wryly observed, will provide 'a puzzle for the excavators of the future'),[18] and behind it placed a bottle containing the names of individuals in the team. A steel door was set within the concrete frame and painted green with a large white stylised 'S' in the centre, not dissimilar to an upside down Superman logo. Steel arches were purchased and placed in position along with timber revetments. Ventilation and lighting were provided by a generator, and after 10 days of round-the-clock shift work the new tunnel broke through into the old one. It was then prepared for the cameras, the floor laid with plywood, and the cameras and lights moved in, along with great lengths of cable to support them, while at the tunnel entrance outside broadcast vehicles were positioned close-by on the edge of the ditch. The process was successful and following an initial live *Chronicle* programme, work on site was suspended until the end of the university term.

Atkinson's green door and logo. (From the Alexander Keiller Museum archive)

Large numbers of people were engaged on various aspects of the work. Arthur Graves and his students from the Geography Department at Bristol University toiled on the slopes, while Lance Vatcher, curator of Avebury Museum, who had been instrumental in carrying out a number of digs for the Ministry of Works, assisted Atkinson and helped supervise the excavation. Archaeology students from Cardiff University, and volunteers from the Wiltshire Archaeological and Natural History Society and elsewhere helped complete the team.

Also in attendance, but rarely mentioned, were various archaeologists' cats and dogs. The note Atkinson left in the portal tells us that Sir Henry de Baskerville, dog, and Ambrose, cat, were present. One of the supervisors, Ken Wilson, who was also an accomplished poet, and his wife Peggy also brought along Honey the cat. As he described, Honey did not make it to the end of the excavation:

> Alas, at Silbury Hill she met her end,
> No more our tent from farm dogs to defend.
> Around the land she travelled far and wide;
> Now peacefully she lies, well stratified.

Clearance of the 1849 tunnel of material was carried out with a small tractor with hydraulic bucket. When, on 5 July, the bucket broke through into the 1849 tunnel, John Taylor, Lance Vatcher and Richard Atkinson crawled in. Most of the roof had collapsed, in one case almost blocking one of the side tunnels, making it necessary to scramble over the piles of fallen material on the tunnel floor. In some places, the sides of the tunnel revealed walls of chalk blocks, and closer to the centre, the deposits were, as Tucker and Merewether had formerly indicated, more complex. Atkinson was astonished to witness the variety of materials and described it as 'a fantastic experience' and like being inside a 'highly coloured layer cake'.[19] Although not having had time to digest what he had seen, once outside he faced the camera. White, shaking and still somewhat awestruck, Atkinson's account was rather incoherent, but it provided the immediacy that would become much valued by television companies.

The section through the mound observed in the walls of the tunnel revealed a buried ditch; it also allowed Atkinson to postulate three main stages of

Richard Atkinson looking into the void above the 1849 tunnel. (From the Alexander Keiller Museum archive)

construction. The first encapsulated a series of events starting with the construction of a small central mound of gravel. This lay on an almost level terrace within the general slope of the chalk spur and was covered by a mound of turf and topsoil that was marked by a series of stakes or posts. Atkinson thought they must have supported a hurdle fence. This was sealed by four complex layers of contrasting black marshy soil, white chalk and coloured flint gravel with an overall diameter of some 34m and reaching an estimated height of just over 5m. Having made measured drawings of the section revealed in the tunnel and made descriptions of the soil layers, this complex series of deposits was labelled Silbury I. Atkinson was amazed at the state of preservation. On removing a portion of turf they were astonished to observe that it was still green, and in the laboratory it was even possible to identify the different species of plants present.

Not only plants but insect remains survived, and later much was made of the ants' wings, thought to indicate the time of year at which this primary phase of the mound was constructed, since ants briefly have wings in early August. It did not take long for these flying ants to become archaeological legend. However, things are rarely as straightforward as they may at first seem, and a recent re-analysis of the 1968/9 insect remains failed to find any winged ants amongst the assemblage; the only evidence being a rather blurred photograph in the Alexander Keiller Museum in Avebury of a slide with parts of ants mounted onto it, including some detached wings, and marked 'Ants found in levels below Silbury Hill'; the slide itself has long since been lost.[20] No winged ants were forthcoming from the recent work either. Furthermore, even if flying ants had been present in the turves, it does not, sadly, give us the month of construction. Professor Mark Robinson of Oxford University, the Silbury insect specialist (or archaeoentomologist to give him his correct title), suggests that it is just as likely that the ants were lying dead in the turves long before becoming incorporated into the mound. As will be seen in Chapter 9, it is important to be clear on this matter: we do not know the time of year that any phase of Silbury was constructed.

Over this organic phase was a large mound of chalk, termed Silbury II, constructed of material that had been extracted from the buried ditch. It reached a diameter of some 73m, but due to the restriction of interpreting deposits visible in the tunnel walls, Atkinson considered that no great time span elapsed between Silbury I and Silbury II, and he believed that in form it was probably conical, a smaller version of Silbury III. The assumed unfinished nature of the buried ditch implied that Silbury III was begun before Silbury II was complete. It involved backfilling the ditch with material dug from a new massive outer ditch and then constructing the enormous mound, some 150m diameter by 31m high, that we see today. This was built up in flat-topped layers, like a wedding cake. The final stage, Silbury IV, was purely aesthetic. Chalk, obtained from the new ditch and its extension to the west, was used to fill in the steps and provide a smoothed profile to the mound. This was thought to have started at the base, but for some reason the uppermost steps were unfinished and left visible.[21]

For the TV audience Atkinson pointed out that the focal point of Silbury I, the centre of the mound, had been disturbed by the shaft sunk in 1776 and that any central burial or other feature that once lay there was now unfortunately beyond reach.

Early in the following year Paul Johnstone of the BBC informed Atkinson that his estimates for ambitious excavation that year had to be cut by 40 per cent. There had been an overspend in 1968 and coupled with an overhaul of the BBC budget there was a need for some economy. Unstated, however, was undoubtedly some disappointment with the results. Ant wings were not exactly the exciting archaeology that some may have been expecting, and there was a general feeling of anti-climax.

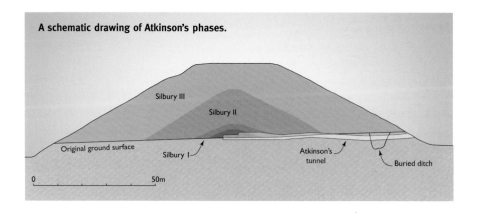

A schematic drawing of Atkinson's phases.

Silbury III

Silbury II

Original ground surface

Silbury I

Atkinson's tunnel

Buried ditch

0   50m

Early in 1969 part of the tunnel collapsed, and this was reported to A J Taylor, Chief Inspector of Monuments at the Ministry of Works. The roof fall then migrated up through the mound to leave a large depression on the surface above the tunnel: 'What happened apparently is that about 60ft above and slightly to the west of the mouth of our new tunnel the unsuspected roof of the Merewether tunnel of 1849 has collapsed, producing a subsidence on the side of the mound about 8ft in diameter and 4ft in depth.'[22] This evidently corresponded with a point in the old tunnel where there had already been a massive pre-1915 collapse in the roof.

On returning to the mound, the roof collapses had to be resolved and new arches inserted where necessary. The tunnel was extended slightly, in doing so encountering the 1776 shaft. At this level it was about 1.5m in diameter and had been excavated for a similar depth into the old ground surface. Atkinson noted that its backfilling contained earthworms, presumably introduced in 1776 (descendants of which were alive and well in 2007). In addition, the side tunnels dug at the instigation of Merewether in 1849 were extended to confirm the extent of the turf mound. The stoneware jar deposited in the centre of the mound in 1849 was recovered in time for an outside broadcast.

Effort then concentrated on a section cut across the south ditch, which was shown to partly underlie the modern road. The inside face of the ditch had been protected from weathering and erosion by a series of stepped deposits of clay and chalk that had protected a wooden revetment. At almost 10m deep, the ditch was an enormous construction and estimated to be 27m wide. Atkinson reported that the high summer temperatures, sometimes of over 90 degrees, were exacerbated by reflection of the sun on the chalk and that salt tablets had to be distributed to the diggers.

On the summit of the mound a rectangular trench revealed the outline of walls comprised of chalk blocks along with a more recent trench that was dated to the 18th century and probably, Atkinson thought, related to the tree-planting episode mentioned by Stukeley. One of the most intriguing finds was a fragment of stone considered to be identical with some of the 'bluestone' at Stonehenge, and at a stroke a link was inferred. Unfortunately, this fragment came from the topsoil rather than a secure archaeological context, and therefore could have been brought to the mound from any date up to the present. A further fragment of stone was recovered, this time from an *in situ* context, but after detailed examination this turned out to be Cornish greenstone, and again any connection with Stonehenge was unwarranted.[23] Further trenches were placed on the upper slopes to investigate the terraces. The upper terrace was considered to have been of Neolithic construction, defined on the inside by a wall of chalk blocks. It was said to have been polished smooth by the feet of workers carrying baskets of chalk rubble.

For its time the work was innovative. Radiocarbon dating, then in its infancy, placed the initial construction at sometime between 2871 and 2486 BC, firmly within the Neolithic period, and broadly contemporary with much of Stonehenge. New approaches in survey had provided photogrammetric contour plans, and geophysical prospection was carried out, along with seismic analysis using a pneumatic hammer. Boreholes were drilled through the mound and ditch so that cores could be studied and ancient deposits analysed in order to determine the nature of the environment.

There were still unresolved problems, and as early as 1 January 1970 Atkinson was planning for a further season. He wrote to A J Taylor:

> Within the guardianship area I am anxious to amplify evidence obtained in 1968 and 1969 in three areas: A) on the flat top of the mound … reopen this cutting in order to examine more fully the plan and structure of these buried walls. B) Half way down the North side of the mound. Here last summer we made a small cutting, 6ft wide by 12ft long, to investigate a slight step or terrace which breaks the smooth profile of the mound at this point. This appeared to have been formed, like other similar terraces higher up the mound, in late Saxon times, possibly for defensive purposes; but below it the cutting revealed what may have been an associated ditch, of which it was possible to excavate only the inner edge. I am anxious to extend this cutting downhill for a limited distance (probably not more than another 12ft) in order to establish

more reliably the character and date of this feature. C) Around the base of the mound. Because of shortage of labour last year (I had to accept a 40% cut in my original estimates) we were not able to trace by excavation the outcrop, near the base of the mound, of the natural chalk spur on which it is built. This information is essential for completeness of description, and for any reliable calculation of the volume of the artificial mound. To obtain this information, I should like to make a small number of trial cuttings, not exceeding ten in number, about 5ft square. I intend also to carry out further borings in the main ditch, in order to amplify information about its profile and filling in the large area where permanent water logging prevents conventional excavation.[24]

The references to the terraces being formed in Saxon times introduced a note of uncertainty in Atkinson's mind that he was presumably keen to resolve. He returned with a small team in 1970 to complete the work on the summit and was able to demonstrate that the chalk rubble matrix of the mound had been revetted by a series of four concentric walls of chalk blocks. But the rest of the programme appears to have suffered from a lack of financial support. He would have liked to have left the tunnel in a well-supported condition so that future access to the centre was retained, but funds had evaporated. The trench through the ditch had already been backfilled and now arrangements were made for the tunnel to be backfilled. Seemingly the decision was made to backfill only the tunnel, leaving the central chamber and lateral tunnels open. Why this decision was taken is unclear; it may have been a compromise between the Ministry of Works and Atkinson's desire to leave it open. Whatever the reason, the Ministry of Works signed off the work, and the green door was slammed shut.

Just before backfilling Paul Johnstone and Ray Kite of the BBC placed a green film box in the back of the tunnel – the BBC's own time capsule. It contained three reels of film in two metal film canisters, a series of paper publications (including publicity pamphlets and a BBC newsletter), the minutes of a meeting held in Devizes, two little lapel badges with the stylised Silbury 'S', and a 50p coin that was brand new when deposited and must have been something of a novelty in a pre-decimalised Britain.

A series of interim reports on the work was prepared and published in the archaeological journal *Antiquity*, and a popular summary appeared in the 1978 BBC book *Chronicle*, edited by Ray Sutcliffe.[25] Archaeologists, however, were eager to get at the detail of the excavation – to see the section drawings and photographs, and to see for themselves the evidence. While Atkinson's methods were innovatory and his interpretations broadly sound, unfortunately a full account of the work did not materialise. Following his death in 1994, much of the work on the mound was eventually admirably published by Alasdair Whittle.[26] By this stage, however, the archive was in a fragmentary state. Nevertheless, description of the mosses, grasses and other plant remains as well as insects and snails from the central mound was made available for the first time. While Atkinson's well-publicised sequence was widely accepted, it was evident, as Whittle himself pointed out, that much greater complexity prevailed.

4 'What do you mean, there's a hole on the top of Silbury?'

The hole that was discovered on the summit of Silbury Hill during the late bank holiday in May 2000 certainly rocked the archaeological establishment. After all, it was akin to a large cavity appearing in one of the Great Pyramids. The hole was almost square and 12m or 13m deep. However, the soil at that depth was thought unlikely to be stable and was possibly an isolated blockage. It was considered to be extremely dangerous, and the chief concern of the National Trust was for public safety. Without delay Amanda Chadburn, an Inspector of Ancient Monuments working for English Heritage, was alerted, as were structural engineers from both the National Trust and English Heritage, the successor organisation to the Ministry of Works. Almost immediately security fencing was erected, while Damian Grady of English Heritage's Aerial Survey team took to the air to take photographs which enabled the situation to be monitored from the skies.

It was quickly realised that the hole represented the shaft excavated in 1776. Aerial photographs of the site taken in 1925 and the 1930s demonstrate that it had been present earlier in the century, and from time to time material within the shaft had slumped and the infill subsequently topped up. The excessive rains of the previous fortnight were thought to have contributed to the collapse, and if they continued (the winter eventually proved to be the wettest on record) could make matters worse. In order to provide some protection a cover of corrugated tin sheeting on a framework of scaffolding was affixed over the hole. A door through the cover allowed inspection of the shaft by lowering individual archaeologists in a harness, and this permitted a certain amount of recording to take place.

The layers visible in the side of the shaft were drawn and photographed. Mining engineers were lowered into the shaft to examine and record it, while English Heritage staff inspected it and took samples for environmental analysis. For archaeologists specialising in prehistory, any trepidation at being lowered into the hole was tempered by sheer excitement at the thought of seeing the interior of one of Europe's most important prehistoric monuments.

The first astonishing thing was that the shaft was square, or nearly so, exactly as the notice in the *Bristol Journal* had stated in 1776,[1] rather than round, and it was so perfectly preserved. As the harness was lowered it was possible to see the uppermost construction of the mound, and at a depth of about 10m, the eastern side of the shaft appeared to change angle as if there were a haul station where spoil could be stored and ladders placed, a gallery or some other feature present. Unfortunately, it was obscured due to the cover of loose soil. It was possible to stand on the soil without it giving way, but it was considered unwise to unstrap the harness.

Archaeologists and the hole

Avebury's very own academic forum, the Avebury Archaeological and Historical Research Group, was quickly informed. This group comprised archaeologists from universities and organisations across the country who had worked on sites in the area, along with local historians and conservationists. The archaeological community was very concerned about the hole; there was uncertainty about the Hill's stability, and, after all, the massive Mississippian Monk's Mound at Cahokia, St Louis, in the United States, had suffered from some subsidence due to water ingress creating slippage of horizontal clay layers, while ziggurats in the Middle East have been equally prone to crumple. While it was swiftly acknowledged that conservation of the Hill and repair of the hole were primary concerns, it was important to establish the relative stability of the rest of the mound. The collapse also presented the opportunity for new archaeological research at Silbury.

Responsibility for conservation of the monument, however, lay with the English Heritage office at Bristol. The task of devising and managing a scheme of remedial works of the mound fell to Rob Harding, but at this stage very little was known about the Hill and it was necessary to arrange surveys, mitigation recording and, potentially, excavation of archaeological deposits before the hole was filled in. Niall Morrissey was Superintendent of Works and responsible for day-to-day matters. He quickly arranged for fencing and security, but as the enormity of the task dawned, the Regional Director quickly established a Project Board in order to recruit the best advice available on how to conserve the site. There was, for example, even concern about exactly what material would be used to fill the hole. Should it be chalk? Or would that obscure the relationship with genuine archaeological deposits? If it were some other material, what kind of chemical and drainage impact would there be on other adjacent deposits?

By the end of July, Fachtna McAvoy and other English Heritage archaeologists based at Fort Cumberland in Portsmouth had photographed, videoed, drawn and described the deposits and along with mining consultants, who carried out a basic survey of the hole, prepared an assessment that incorporated recommendations for excavation and recording around the lip of the shaft. At this stage the mound was considered stable, and it was simply necessary to record the archaeology adequately and backfill the hole with appropriate material.

The year 2000 held a further twist. During part of a regular inspection early in December, it was noticed that the sides of the shaft had caved in and fresh archaeological deposits were visible. The summit was less stable than previously thought and, as if to emphasise this, little more than a week later there was a further collapse. The hole was now 5m × 7m, although much material from the sides had collapsed into the shaft, partly filling it, but nevertheless leaving a crater almost 4m deep. In addition, an area of slumped material some 4m wide lay on the south-west side of the hole. It was evident that the cover was not serving its purpose and may indeed have been influencing drainage, with its weight providing a destabilising downward force and making matters worse. As a result it was removed just before Christmas and a higher fence erected to deter the over-curious.

Aerial photograph of the mound taken just months after the first collapse showing the further subsidence. The outline left by the corrugated tin cover can be clearly seen, while a further cave-in is about to occur. (NMR 21034/24)

Following this new collapse, structural engineers were less confident about the stability of the mound. Atkinson had formerly observed that material had fallen from the roof of the 1849 tunnel and that this material was replaced by deposits from further up; the void had effectively migrated to the surface. It was quite possible that other parts of the tunnel, particularly the extensive 1849 digging in the central area, were similarly migrating upwards towards the surface of the mound. The mound could have been riddled with voids, as the English Heritage press release put it, a little like a 'Swiss cheese'. Theoretically, the earlier tunnels had been backfilled to the roof, but it was not possible to be certain. There was similar concern about any modern backfilling aimed at plugging the 2000 hole, which might only temporarily mask any voids in the Hill. Indeed, should there be further voids at a lower point in the shaft, the sheer weight of backfilled material might cause more collapses. It was therefore considered essential to try to establish the extent of the problem and take measures to resolve it, rather than simply trying to patch up the visible damage.

Early in the New Year, a geophysical survey of the summit was carried out by the team from Fort Cumberland. Several scientific prospection techniques were used – electrical resistivity, magnetometry, and radar surveys – to try and ascertain what lay beneath the surface. The results, when plotted on a computer screen, revealed a number of anomalies. While these techniques identified features up to severalmetres below the surface, the work served to highlight the desirability of geophysical prospection of the mound as a whole. No such survey had been attempted within the archaeological world before, yet it was important to know whether further cavities existed deeper within the mound that might lead to further collapse. Would it be possible? Surveys using seismic refraction or reflection might work.

A cutting-edge, high-tech method of seismic recording was available from the United States; this provided a computerised image of the interior of the mound and was soon commissioned. The process involved drilling holes through the mound from the summit to the base, pumping in water and setting off airgun charges, responses from which could be recorded at different depths by equipment set on the slopes around the mound. The signal would then allow soils of different densities to be measured and plotted as a computer-generated 3D model of the interior of the mound, thus highlighting any anomalies, cavities or other features that it contained. However, for this a drill rig would need to be hoisted to the summit and placed alongside the hole in exactly the position where deposits were considered to be potentially unstable. In other words, such an exercise could only be carried out after the hole had been backfilled, which would rather negate the whole point of the exercise.

The answer was to temporarily fill the hole to make the summit stable enough for the seismic survey to take place, but allow for renewed access should other cavities be discovered. The advantage of this solution was that it would also protect the top of the shaft from further damage from the weather. However, this simply introduced a further complication, namely that preparing the summit in this way could damage deposits around the lip of the hole. Consequently, in May 2001 two small excavation trenches were cut on the summit, placed either side of the crater and aimed at testing the deposits that were exposed in the collapsed shaft, along with the adjacent anomalies highlighted in the geophysical survey. The recovery of medieval pottery and metalwork and a Roman coin highlighted the lengthy use of the summit of the Hill, but a chalk wall over 2m wide with a fragment of red deer antler hard against it indicated that prehistoric features were definitely present at this level.

A plan of the site and a plan of action

Analytical investigation of the site and its environs was carried out involving topographical survey of the subtle surface undulations. In addition, the use of survey-grade GPS allowed calculation of the volume of the mound to be made, the first modern estimate of its size. It reached a maximum of 31m in height, had a variable diameter at the base of between 135m and 145m and comprised over 239,000 cubic metres of chalk, most of which could have derived from the surrounding ditch and its extension (from which some 235,500 cubic metres of material could have been extracted). Coupled with documentary research into the former archaeological work, the historical background and land use, the survey helped to explain the role and use of the features on and around the mound. In addition, a photogrammetric plot was prepared from aerial photographs taken in 1968 so that it could be compared to the new surveys to ascertain whether any surface movement was noticeable. Careful observation of the surface earthworks resulted in a series of plans that not only allowed the mound and surrounding landscape to be digitally modelled in 3D, but ensured a greater understanding of its development.

The topographical survey was undertaken in two stages during May and June 2001, the break being necessary because of the level of water that was retained in the ditch until relatively late in the year and because of restrictions in movement that had been imposed following an outbreak of Foot and Mouth amongst cattle. This highly contagious disease caused great disruption locally. Bales of disinfected straw were spread across the roads into local villages and farms, access to many of the local footpaths were forbidden to visitors, and the sudden visits dreaded by famers from DEFRA, the government organisation responsible, cast a shadow over the Marlborough Downs. Few herds were hit, but there were restriction zones, and the smell of disinfectant was ubiquitous. The sight of smoke drifting across the chalk at Broad Hinton sickened.

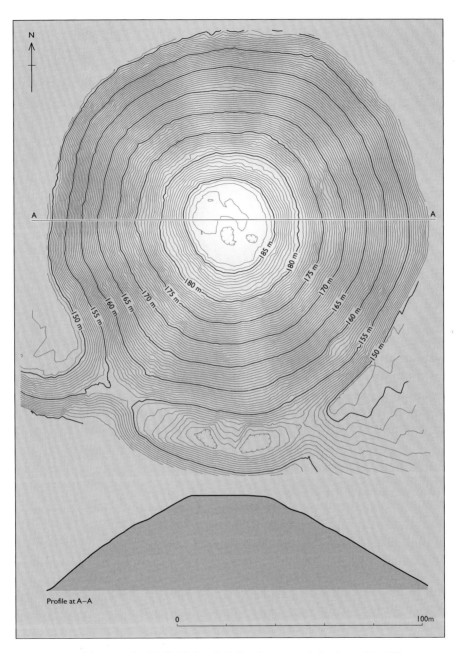

Contour plan of the mound, with highlights depicting the segmented nature of the Hill.

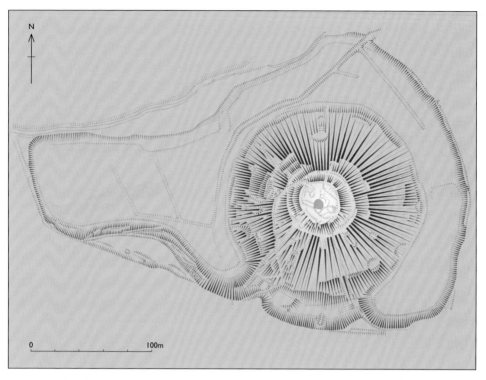

Hachured plan of Silbury Hill. The hachures represent slopes which are broken by a series of terraces and platforms all providing detail of construction episodes and indications of past use. Note, in particular, the earthworks on the summit.

The public and the hole

While archaeologists and conservationists were struggling with the mechanics of the Hill, there were other concerns to resolve. Despite initial attempts by the National Trust and English Heritage to keep things low-key and not attract undue attention, word very quickly got round that a hole had appeared, and the excitement of being able to see the interior of the mound proved a temptation. It was a topic of conversation in the region's pubs, and with mobile phones and the internet providing speedy communication rumours were rife. Arthur McCallum, conservation engineer, had lowered a video camera down the shaft to obtain film for English Heritage, but Dutch visitors had also managed to jump over the fence and climb down a rope with a camera. They quickly put their video on the internet.

By the middle of June 2000 larger than usual numbers had gathered for the summer solstice, and on the morning of the 21st one traveller reported that her partner, last seen scaling the mound the night before, was missing. A full-scale alert involving the Wiltshire Fire Brigade resulted in him being found asleep on the summit beneath the corrugated tin sheeting, accompanied by an empty bottle of parsnip and banana wine. The incident served to emphasise the potential danger, and security guards were subsequently positioned at the base of the Hill. Such problems inevitably placed an increased financial and organisational burden on the National Trust, who were in any case at full stretch to manage the estate, particularly at significant dates in the solar calendar such as Midsummer Day. Although the Hill is owned by the 4th Baron Avebury, a descendant of John Lubbock, it is in the guardianship of the Secretary of State for the Department for Culture, Media and Sport who had given this role to English Heritage. English Heritage had, in turn, passed the management of the monument to the National Trust who own and manage other pieces of land nearby, including the Avebury stone circles. Since the collapse on the summit, English Heritage resumed this responsibility for Silbury Hill. A press release emphasised that it was essential to map all the cavities, known and unknown, before repairs were carried out and that excavation on the summit was to ensure its stability so that a drill rig could be put in place, preliminary to carrying out the 3D seismic survey.

A newspaper headline announcing the hole. (Photo: Brian Edwards. Courtesy of WANHS)

While information on the stability of the mound was being gathered on which to determine an appropriate conservation response, the lack of visible activity and the apparent silence from English Heritage was proving disconcerting for some members of the public. The *Wiltshire Gazette & Herald* reported public fears that unless English Heritage took urgent remedial action the 'actual rim of the hill could subside'.[2] The case was taken up by Lord Avebury, who wrote to both Lord McIntosh, heritage spokesman in the House of Lords and also to Michael Ancram, MP for Devizes; the latter in turn spoke to Sir Neil Cossons, then Chairman of English Heritage, calling for speedy action. Days later there were more headlines, such as 'Rescue plan as ancient hill collapses',[3] in which English Heritage was quoted as re-emphasising the programme, but explanations of a cutting-edge seismic survey to establish the extent of the problem did not wash with some sections of the public.

With the first anniversary of the discovery of the collapse approaching, Avebury resident Pete Glastonbury, along with Clare Slaney and representatives from the Ancient Sacred Landscapes Network, Pagan Federation and Druid Orders, organised a peaceful protest to try and get English Heritage to take steps to conserve the mound and act with transparency, while communicating with the concerned public. Clare Slaney was quoted in *The Times Higher Education Supplement* as saying that delays by English Heritage had 'put the hill in jeopardy' and compared the neglect to destruction by the Taliban.[4] One idea was to get enough people to encircle the base of Silbury and link arms. It was, however, realised that the precautions necessary for the Foot and Mouth epidemic had to be respected and so would preclude such action. On the day 25 or so people showed up and completed a protest march from Avebury to Silbury, but the 'Battle of Silbury Hill', as *The Times Magazine* called it,[5] continued, with a particular emphasis being on the lack of transparency and absence of information coming out of English Heritage. Daggers were drawn, with only thinly disguised barbs from some conservationists aimed at Amanda Chadburn, the English Heritage representative. As she had done with countless newspaper reporters, Amanda stood her ground and re-emphasised the reason for care and caution. The issues were complex and involved intricate health and safety matters, as well as the safeguarding of extremely important and fragile archaeological deposits.

Problems were anticipated at the 2001 summer solstice by English Heritage, and preparations were made for an all-night presence at the mound. In previous years, the event had been managed successfully by the National Trust in a low-key non-confrontational manner. While the police ensured that there was no parking or obstruction of the A4, National Trust staff traditionally maintained a visible presence and asked people to respect the site and not trespass on the Hill. The open hole on the summit made it particularly important that no-one was able to scale the fence, especially in the dark. Offerings of flowers, candles, turf and other deposits were often placed in and around the lip of the crater, so the problem was a very real one. The controversy in the press also brought a significant amount of attention to the site and a higher than usual number of visitors was expected. English Heritage staff, including Regional Director Kevin Brown and Amanda Chadburn, took shifts to turn away would-be visitors to the summit. Visitors were instead asked to respect the Hill, and most went away peacefully and contentedly. Several individuals in a camper van arrived at 11.30 pm and said that they were an advance party of a group of 10,000 shamans who had arranged to hold a service on the summit at 2.00 am and that they had permission for the event from the Regional Head of English Heritage. They were duly pointed in the direction of the said Head, who stood just yards away, but the shaman decided to leave and go to Stonehenge instead. The anticipated flood of people did not arrive, and by dawn it was clear that Stonehenge had provided a greater attraction. Nobody had fallen down the hole, and the only event of note was an individual who was caught spread-eagled on the upper terrace of the mound in the police helicopter searchlight. In the dark he had evaded the security around the base of the mound, but after scaling the Hill he was found to be flat out, the worse for drink and fast asleep.

The protest and police presence at Silbury in June 2001. (Photo: Brian Edwards. Courtesy of WANHS)

In the meantime ...

The temporary polystyrene filling. (AA027554)

The deposits exposed in the sides of the new crater were recorded and then lined with a geotextile membrane and filled with large polystyrene blocks subsequently weighted down with 50 tonnes of chalk. Each 1-tonne bag of chalk was carefully lifted by helicopter from the field to the east of Silbury and, watched by a small interested gathering of local people, was dropped on to the polystyrene to make the surface stable and secure. Each time the bag was released the helicopter leapt visibly into the air. Ros Cleal, National Trust archaeologist and curator of the

The helicopter dumping chalk on the summit of Silbury Hill. (AA012338)

The drill rig being taken up Silbury Hill. (AA027603)

Alexander Keiller Museum at Avebury later recalled how the polystyrene gave the summit an uncanny feeling. It appeared to shudder if you jumped on it as though the Hill was made of jelly.

Skanska, the appointed construction contractors, hoisted the drill rig to the summit and it was carefully assembled and set up adjacent to the crater. Four holes were bored right through the mound to the natural chalk below. The resulting cores, each some 50m long, provided a superb vertical section of the deposits through the mound. They were saved and transported in sections to Fort Cumberland, Portsmouth, where the English Heritage archaeological laboratories are located, for detailed archaeological analysis. The fourth core inadvertently encountered a void at a depth of a little over 27m, and a camera was put down the hole. It was evident that the void was one of Atkinson's lateral tunnels. It was also clear from the picture that no backfilling of this part of the tunnel had taken place, and the upper part of the supporting steel arches was visible, but standing free. The roof material had collapsed on to the tunnel floor, and the roof had begun to migrate upwards. A fifth hole was drilled to compensate, but the suspicions were confirmed; there were indeed other cavities that could produce problems in the future.

The data from the seismic survey were sent back to the United States for processing and analysis, from which two-dimensional images of selected planes through the mound were prepared, along with three-dimensional models of the interior of the Hill.

The Project Board met early in July 2002 to hear Mark Kirkbride of Skanska present the initial results. The results were intriguing but also confusing and, as with traditional geophysical plots, considerable importance was attached to the skills of interpretation. Important anomalies were visible in the area of Atkinson's tunnels, and while the central shaft that had caused the initial problem appeared to have been filled to a reasonable level, there was a significant irregularity visible at the centre. One anomaly was noted on the northern slopes which

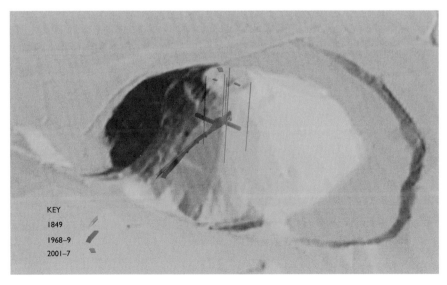

KEY
1849
1968–9
2001–7

Locations of the 2000 to 2008 work, including boreholes, tunnel and the trenches on the summit.

correlated with that identified on the surface by the analytical survey, and this was given particular emphasis. According to the seismic survey, it extended for some 10m below the surface, and as discussion progressed this became known as 'the northern anomaly'. There were clearly unresolved problems in this area and it was felt that more information was required here.

No clear structures were revealed in the base of chalk, but a number of anomalies appeared at ground level, some of which corresponded with the known buried ditch. Others, however, appeared to descend to considerable depths and could only be explained as geological in nature. The images were appealing, but given the exploratory nature of the survey it was of the ultimate necessity to establish the degree of confidence that could be ascribed to them. The results needed to be robust and resilient under scrutiny. The methodology involved potential causes of error relating to sound travel time or uneven ray coverage, and Professors Michael Worthington and Richard Chandler from Imperial College, University of London, assessed the results. They concluded that the mound itself was essentially rather homogenous. Worthington considered that there was no major risk to the stability of the hill, while Chandler agreed that no major voids had been revealed by the survey, but that the void identified in the core hole could develop and migrate, or it may stabilise. However, seismic ray coverage in the central area was poor and the results were considered unreliable, and so he suggested that further detail of this area was also needed. In contrast, the results and interpretation of the northern anomaly were acceptable but needed further definition. Clarity was needed in both areas, and Skanska were consequently asked to refine their survey, which they did. The seismic survey was conducted between boreholes as well as from the central boreholes to the outer slope of the mound in order to provide greater detail of that area. The second attempt produced similar conclusions, namely that low-velocity anomalies existed below the central crater, around the entrance to Atkinson's tunnel, as well as on the lower northern slopes.

The 'northern anomaly' was intriguing, and a surface-based refraction survey was therefore conducted across it. While this confirmed the earlier results it provided significantly different measurements. Nevertheless, it was now felt that

A hole on the top of Silbury?

geophysical methods had been taken as far as possible in terms of investigating these features. Professor Chandler felt that a cutting across the 'northern anomaly' might resolve matters. Subsequently, it was agreed that Fachtna McAvoy should place a trench across it in order to try to resolve its nature. In the event some further localised coring was carried out. Four cores were obtained across the feature by Matt Canti, a soil scientist based at Fort Cumberland. These revealed a marked contrast in the deposits, which were considered to be consistent with an infilled feature. While the question of what this was remained, attention turned back to the central area.

Further sampling of the central area was then commissioned to investigate whether voids existed within or adjacent to the shaft. In particular one chimney-shaped void alongside the shaft gave concern. Two new boreholes were drilled, one in the shaft and one through the chimney adjacent to it. The former encountered no voids until it struck a stanchion in Atkinson's tunnel and encountered a considerable void at that level. A camera was lowered down the hole, and the void was estimated to be over 1.5m deep, and it could be seen to extend away from the camera for at least 4m. The latter, however, revealed no evidence for a void. This could be, as Skanska suggested, the result of changes in chalk saturation or other subtleties, but nevertheless illustrated the importance of caution highlighted in Professor Worthington's work.

The process had of necessity taken a considerable period of time, as the results of one investigation posed questions that led to another piece of work, but was deemed to have been worthwhile, although the results, rigorously analysed by Professors Chandler and Worthington were difficult to interpret. Generally they showed that the mound was essentially stable, but that its condition would deteriorate if the tunnels and shaft were not backfilled. There were various options ranging from 'do nothing' to installing a further temporary cap over the shaft. It was possible to drill into and pump material into the voids if one could be certain that they had all been identified, although there would be no means of checking whether any grouting had completely filled the area intended. In any case, there was uncertainty about the longer-term chemical effect of such grouting. The final and more complete option was to re-excavate and make safe the shaft and tunnels, either by shoring them if they were to be kept open or by backfilling in order to conserve the mound. A comprehensive report on the various available options and their respective conservation impact was prepared by Fachtna McAvoy and set before the Project Team.

The conclusions were pointing to the necessity of a major intervention, and the archaeologists were beginning to shift around on their seats with increasing optimism, not to say excitement, at the prospect of this. Archaeologists and others with an interest were invited to a meeting in Devizes to hear a series of presentations on the work to date and to provide comment on the best way forward, and implications of each of the options were considered. Prominent archaeologists, including Professor Richard Bradley and Professor Peter Fowler, recognised the nature of the conservation issue, but also emphasised the imperative of the research opportunity that would never again be encountered in our lifetime. It should, they felt, be grasped with both hands. Having considered the various strands of advice along with the survey evidence, it was concluded that there was no real option but to re-enter the tunnel. Of course it would cost a lot to do this, but the final decision rested with the English Heritage Advisory Committee. Rob Harding duly made his report. In 2006 authorisation was given for the work to go ahead, and the scene was set for a major investigation.

5 Creating the mound

'They're wrong again,' crackled the radio. 'You need to re-survey that stretch of the tunnel.' There appeared to be something wrong with the Total Station Theodolite. Every day a new stretch of the tunnel was surveyed and the data sent back to the office in the compound to be downloaded and compared with the previous day's survey. Archaeologists would then radio back to the tunnel to say that they matched, and work could then continue. But by the end of July 2007 this stopped working smoothly; the stretches of the tunnel would not join up. In time honoured fashion it was the tools that were first blamed, and a new theodolite was introduced, but still the problem persisted.

In hindsight it was blindingly obvious. When the tunnel was constructed in the 1960s, the roof was high to allow clearance for machinery. In 2007 it served a similar purpose, and also allowed both miners and archaeologists to walk through the tunnel with hard hats on without stooping. But it happened slowly, insidiously, over a week. So slowly that it was not noticed. The taller individuals started catching the top of their hard hats on the tunnel roof – just skimming the very top – barely noticeable, but bit by bit, day by day, more of the hats banged on the arches. After a week of this, coupled with the consistent survey errors, realisation dawned: the arches in the middle of the mound were slowly sinking into the ground. This part of the tunnel was slowly collapsing, and this was why the survey points were not matching – the whole arch system was moving.

Over the following week the central part of the tunnel continued to collapse. Archaeological work all but stopped, and the miners did what they could to prevent loose chalk flowing into localised parts of the tunnel. The arches had sunk so much in the centre that it was necessary to bend down when walking along the middle stretch of the tunnel, and some of the arches had begun to twist and buckle under the strain. It rained a lot in 2007 – in fact it was one of the wettest summers on record. The rain had permeated through the chalk, making it heavier, sloppier and more mobile; and all this contributed to the collapse.

Going in

In May 2007, a few weeks before this collapse occurred, Skanska had arrived in the field to the east of Silbury and started to set up their offices and sleeping quarters. The miners and engineers slept on site for the duration in self-contained cabins – rectangular steel boxes, complete with their own en-suite facilities. Another large rectangular box formed the canteen – this contained a sink, oven and fridge, cupboards, tables and benches, and was used by everyone on site. Male and female toilets were also brought in. Along with offices for the engineers and archaeologists, there was a finds processing hut, storage facilities and changing rooms; with roads running between the buildings, the field had become an active but temporary village. A platform was constructed around the entrance of the tunnel (which had been previously located and exposed), and this platform area became known as the portal.

Once the portal was ready and the 1968 door had been fully exposed, the team began to gear up for the grand opening, and the excitement was tangible. On Friday 11 May 2007, the large green door that had been closed nearly 40 years previously was opened. A large Yale padlock hung from the door – it was removed using bolt cutters, but once the door had been opened, the corresponding key was found on the floor on the other side; the door had been locked in 1970 and the key simply posted under it (presumably with some humour). The press had been invited of course; this was, after all, to be English Heritage's flagship excavation. In the event they seemed more interested in the Druids, who had turned up in all manner of attire, but the official opening was covered in most of the major papers and spirits were high.

Upon opening the door, the first people to enter were greeted by collapsed chalk from the tunnel roof, mixed with roadstone and a jumble of other things such as decayed wood and rubber tyres. A small tracked vehicle trundled up a scaffold ramp and made its way to the portal so that it could clear this material. Once removed, it could be seen that the tunnel had been filled with pink, Type 1 roadstone. The roadstone was loose and clearly had not been fully compacted when blown into the tunnel in 1970, and therefore provided little support to the tunnel roof. As the wooden boards that formed the tunnel roof rotted away in the years following the backfilling, chalk from the overlying mound collapsed into the tunnel, compressing the roadstone by about one-third. This collapsed chalk and roadstone was removed using a small machine with a bucket on the front that lumbered its way in and out of the tunnel under the supervision of an archaeologist. The chalk was taken back to the compound and loaded onto a conveyor belt so that it could be searched for finds by a team of eager archaeologists.

Atkinson's steel mining arches were present throughout the tunnel and were still marked with the numbers his team had painted on to them; this meant that it was possible to retain his numbering system, with the arch number referring to the stretch of tunnel immediately after it (known as a bay). Since most of the arches were upright (except in the central area around the 1776 shaft, where they were leaning but still stable), they were reused, but the roof lining, which had entirely rotted away, was replaced with metal plates. As well as the arches, a few other objects relating to Atkinson's tunnelling works were found, and these included metal braces used in the construction of the tunnel, an iron pick end (although this is possibly from the earlier 1849 tunnelling works), a large spanner and a plumb bob. Three tobacco tins were found just outside the tunnel in the portal area, which presumably belonged to some of the 1960s miners or archaeologists who had left them in a convenient position at the tunnel entrance so that they could nip out for a smoke now and again and, for whatever reason, just never picked them up at the end of the site.

The conditions in the tunnel were far from ideal for archaeological recording; it was cramped and despite the ventilation tubes the air was foul and the lighting poor at best. It was under these difficult conditions that the deposits that form the mound visible in the tunnel sides were recorded. Conventionally the section would be hand-drawn, but given the conditions and pressures of working in the tunnel (bearing in mind that the tunnel was shared with the miners), a technique was needed that was as accurate as it was easy to use. The solution was to record the archaeology visible in the sides using stereo-photography – this involved placing visible markers where they would appear in the photos and surveying them using a Total Station Theodolite (an accurate surveying instrument) to provide fixed control points from which to record. The arches were strong; they had supported the tunnel for the last 40 years and were the obvious place

Archaeologist Ellie Leary recording part of the sequence in the tunnel (foreground) with miners and engineers working in background, showing how closely the archaeologists and miners worked together. (661-7137-02)

How the tunnel looked following the July 2007 collapse. (661-6144-04)

to locate these fixed control points. Two photographs were then taken of the same area, about 300mm apart, with a digital camera. These photographs and the survey information could then be put into a computer program, which (effectively replicating what your eyes do) created a three-dimensional image of each bay. The survey information allowed each bay to be stitched together on the computer, and, as if by magic, a single, three-dimensional tunnel side was produced – the Silbury tunnel in virtual reality.

Following the July collapse it took a number of weeks for Skanska to stabilise the tunnel again. Some of the arches were completely sealed in by collapsed material, while others were twisted and broken. New arches had to be procured to replace the few that had been lost or damaged, and the miners began re-tunnelling again – frustratingly, through areas that had previously been exposed. It had delayed the project schedule, but in the meantime the planned excavations on the summit were brought forward, which involved digging a small trench 3m × 5m, and which overlapped slightly with Atkinson's previous trench.

Jim Leary and Terry Hilton (the head miner) celebrating when the back of the tunnel was finally reached. (661-7139-03)

Back in the tunnel, work continued as before and this time without a hitch, and the full tunnel including both lateral tunnels was finally exposed and recorded. The end of the tunnel was reached on 27 September and was a joyous occasion for the miners and archaeologists who had toiled so hard to get there. A small surprise waited: lying right at the back of the tunnel was a green metal box with a wooden inner lining and bearing the BBC insignia. This was the BBC's time capsule from 1969.

With the tunnel now open it was possible to see, in its sides, the development of the mound. And by moving out from the earliest phases in the centre, towards the portal, it was possible to interpret the site as growing, enlarging, changing and maturing.

Before the mound

Visible in the sides at about waist height was a deposit that represents the former Neolithic ground level – a thin, grey band of silty clay with a smooth, buttery consistency. It was distinct and obvious – below it was natural geology: chalk bedrock overlain by a mixture of clay and flints, known, imaginatively, as clay-with-flints. Above this were the materials that form the mound itself. When Falkner and Blandford dug their tunnel in 1849 they immediately recognised this band as the old ground level and purposely kept it visible in the tunnel sides at about 500mm below the roof level so that any evidence of a grave could easily be seen. When Atkinson re-opened this tunnel he also noted the same grey band. But at only a few millimetres it is too thin to be the full Neolithic soil horizon. Following Atkinson's work, this was explained as the result of compression; the sheer weight of the overlying mound forcing out all the pockets of air that exist within cracks and earthworm holes in the soil. But this explanation does not stand scrutiny: the topsoil and subsoil would have been between 200mm and 300mm thick before compaction; regardless of the weight being applied to it, it could never compress down to just a few millimetres. In addition, the band was almost entirely devoid of stones.

The pre-mound activity.

There must be another way of explaining this thin, stone-free band, and Matt Canti, the soil scientist working on the project, wondered if part of the soil could have been stripped away at some point before a monument even existed on the site. Digging away the soil like this could have left the top of the subsoil exposed, and perhaps with people and animals walking up and down on this sticky, muddy surface, and indeed with earthworms turning and churning the soil, it may not have been long before the thin band of mud seen in the tunnel sides began to take shape.

The idea that the ground could have been prepared before any construction had begun would profoundly affect our understanding of the origins of the site, suggesting that the location had already seen considerable activity before monument construction began. If the Hill already attracted people, it may have already been special, perhaps even sacred, ground. Further evidence for pre-mound activity came from the work in the centre of the tunnel, where lying within the stripped surface was the edge of a small, scorched patch of ground, crammed with charcoal and a few charred hazel nutshells. This is the remains of an ancient hearth. Two burnt pig teeth lay amongst the charcoal; relics from a Neolithic meal, or perhaps part of a sacrificial or ceremonial event.

The site therefore was already drawing people to it before the mound was built; it was a place of considerable activity. And if, as is likely to have been the case, this land was strewn with naturally occurring sarsen stones, the area must have been cleared of these stones before or while the turf and topsoil was being stripped away. This may well have given the appearance of an enclosure, much as a patch of cleared woodland would, with sarsen boulders pulled to the edge of the area and either purposefully or unintentionally demarcating it.

The earliest mound

Deep inside the tunnel, by carefully peeling away the collapsed material that adhered to the sides, it was possible in the fluorescent light to make out, dull, golden, sticky gravel resting on top of the stripped surface. The gravel had clearly been piled up into a small round mound a little less than 1m high and nearly 10m in diameter; hardly a worthy predecessor to the giant mound we see today, but a mound nonetheless. People had clearly gone to some effort to construct this, as the gravel had been brought on to the site, perhaps from the River Kennet, or picked

The earliest mound.

from the clay-with-flints that covers the natural underlying ground. This effort suggests that the gravel had been specifically chosen for the task at hand and was perhaps considered special.

Pieces of place

We cannot now tell how long this diminutive Silbury stood proud – days, weeks or perhaps years, but what could be clearly seen in the damp and musty tunnel sides was that, at some stage, it was enlarged. A ring of stakes had been hammered into the ground to define the perimeter of a larger 16-metre area around the gravel mound. Individual loads of mud and dark soils, probably carried in baskets or hides, had been tipped into this space to create a mound

The organic mound surrounded by stakes.

Hairy Garden Snail
Trichia hispida

Glass Snail
Vitrina pellucida

Plaited Door Snail
Cochlodina laminata

that was about waist high. The deposit was made predominantly from topsoil and subsoil but also contained turves – the grass and moss still visible on them. This may well have been the soil that was stripped from the ground before construction began, particularly since this soil is clayey in nature, which equates with the clay-with-flints geology found in the immediate vicinity. It may well be that this soil, once stripped, was stored nearby before being used in the mound.

This was not the only area to have seen mound construction – a few metres away to the south and south-east, two smaller mounds were visibly outlined in the section, and others may well exist beyond the confines of the tunnel. Made from dark organic mud, these two small mounds stood less than half a metre high. They were not natural features but deliberately constructed mounds that were added to and modified over time, and one even had a tiny gully dug around it; like a small-scale model of the final Silbury. This is an entirely new discovery, and we can now say that the early phases of Silbury do not comprise just one monument, but a number of them that later became subsumed into a single form.

The soils from all these early mounds preserved organic material astonishingly well, giving us a graphic snapshot of the state of the local environment. Insects are so staggeringly well preserved that to Richard Atkinson, commenting on his discoveries in *The Listener* magazine in January 1969, they looked 'so lifelike that it is difficult to believe that a prod with the dissecting needle will not send them scuttling for cover'.[1] The majority of the insects come from open grassland, indicating that this environment predominated when Silbury was being constructed. There is an abundance of weevils and some leaf beetles too, as well as a variety of dung beetles, which feed on the droppings of animals such as cow and sheep. Other beetles include the predatory snail-eating beetle, the sexton beetle, which buries small, dead animals and birds for its larvae to feed on, the devil's coach horse, a single green tiger beetle and a shield bug. These insects indicate that the climate was much the same as it is today.

Grass and moss are still green, and it is not difficult to imagine the grass blades waving in the wind. The seeds and plant remains confirm the evidence from the insects that these early mounds were set in a mature, well-grazed grassland,

Garden Chafer
Phyllopeptha horticola

Green Tiger Beetle
Cicindela Campest

Silpha atrata

although one of the mini-mounds preserved remains more associated with woodland or scrub, since it contained yew berries, sloe stones, hazel nutshell fragments and bramble seeds, and perhaps the soil for this mound had been collected from a different place to the others. The vivid picture we get of the later Neolithic countryside surrounding Silbury is a mosaic of meadows for pasture and patches of woodland, which may well have been managed in some way, while cereal chaff in one of the mini-mounds may provide us with evidence for small-scale agriculture as well.

BLACKBERRY

Mound building stops

Manipulation of the site temporarily changed emphasis at this point, and rather than adding material, pits were dug into the top and side of the central organic mound. Two were recorded in the tunnel sides, although others no doubt exist beyond that. These pits were not large – around one metre in diameter and depth. As much of these pits as possible was archaeologically excavated. However, there was little in them that could provide any clue to their original purpose; even their fill seems to have been little more than the dug-out material pushed back in. There were, however, some fragments of worked flint at the bottom, and one pit contained an army of worker ants signifying the inclusion, perhaps inadvertently, of a turf containing an ant nest. Lying, as they do, on the top and side of the mound, it is hard to believe that these pits had any practical function, but are more likely to be the result of ceremonial activity on and around the mound.

Rubra myrinic nest.

... and then resumes

Mound assembly continued, and these pits, along with the organic mounds, became sealed under dumps of different material that had been tipped over the top. This was made up from basket-loads of topsoil, chiefly gathered from soil that directly overlay chalk, and therefore from beyond the immediate clay-with-flints area (and contrasting with the far more locally derived underlying mound), as well as basket-loads of chalk, clay, gravel and more turf. Again, turning to Richard Atkinson's evocative descriptions helps to conjure the image of a cross-section through these multi-coloured and interleaved layers: 'Seen in section, these upper layers have a stripe pattern, like a polychrome tiger's skin, the white chalk contrasting sharply with the dark-grey soil and the yellows and browns of the gravel and clay.'[2] Together, these layers formed a mound with an estimated diameter of 35m and which was perhaps as high as 5m or 6m, although

Archaeologists Ellie Leary and James Cooper study the 'polychrome tiger's skin' of the organic mound at the very end of the tunnel. (661-7143-03)

this will never be known for sure, as it extended well above the tunnel and so the top could not be seen. Not only were soils used to create this larger mound; a number of naturally rounded sarsen boulders were present as well. But these were not displayed as a setting on top or as a basal stone circle around it, as one might imagine and indeed as Tucker and Merewether reported.[3] Rather, they had been deliberately incorporated within the body of the mound as an element of its composition – or as Magnús Magnússon eloquently put it during one of the *Chronicle* films, the sarsens were 'seeded right through the primary mound like raisins in a cake'.[4] The material for these early mounds had been carefully chosen; this was no random spoil heap, but pieces of other places carefully piled high.

The white mound

Once this intricate stack had been piled up, chalk was then added. In the sides of the tunnel could be seen five banks of chalk, sometimes mixed with clay, which, if extended, would have formed rings around the earlier monument; each new ring gently expanding the monument outwards by a few more metres at a time. We do not know what role these banks had, particularly since the tops of some of them extended above the tunnel and were therefore hidden from view. Perhaps the banks were part of a larger construction process, with the material engulfing the earlier organic mound and forming successively larger white mounds. Or perhaps these banks formed distinct and separate phases of activity, each one being formed around the inner mound, which was probably not covered over with chalk, but remained visible.

Some of these chalk banks had been mixed with clay giving them a light brown appearance, with lumps of chalk and clay separately appearing as little white and brown nuggets. In his notebook, Atkinson compared this particular mix with the chocolate bar Toblerone[5] – a far more apt description than the characterless 'light yellow brown' that recording systems force the modern archaeologists to use today. Indeed, Atkinson often appears to have used food metaphors – on one occasion he described Silbury Hill as 'an enormously complicated and highly-coloured layer cake' and as a 'wedding-cake',[6] and in *The Listener* the organic mound formed 'a kind of enormous biological club sandwich'.[7] It was as if he quite literally wanted to devour the deposits.

The chalk rubble and clay for these banks are likely to have been quarried from a large surrounding ditch, the evidence for which could be seen just inside the entrance in the tunnel sides and below the tunnel floor. Here the tunnel floor was archaeologically excavated to the bottom of the ditch in order to glimpse as complete a profile as possible. And it was large: over 6.5m deep and 6m wide, and, assuming the ditch was circular in plan, it would have formed an enclosure around the monument over 100m in diameter. On the inner lip of the ditch was a bank over 1m high and made from Atkinson's Toblerone. The Neolithic quarry workers had clearly used picks made from red deer antler to extract the hard chalk, and by hammering the point of the pick into cracks and fissures in the chalk were able to prise lumps out. It is assumed here that this ditch had been dug around the earlier phases of activity described above, since the chalk quarried from the ditch was piled against it. However, it may well be that there had been an enclosing ditch from the earliest phase.

The section of the Neolithic ditch that extended below the tunnel floor under excavation. It was necessary to shore the sides of the trench in order to prevent collapse. (661-6282-01)

Creating the mound

Either way it is important to realise that at one point in its use, Silbury was a well-defined bank and ditch enclosure; it was open and presumably accessible, the opposite of our classic understanding of the monument as a mounded space. There are other monuments that resemble the Silbury Enclosure: the first phase of Stonehenge, for example, which, although much earlier, also consisted of a ditch with a low internal bank. There are also similarities with an enclosure excavated in Dorchester, Dorset, called the Flagstones Enclosure, that was likewise a little over 100m in diameter. Perhaps Silbury Hill and these other sites had more in common than their final manifestations suggest.

The Silbury ditch was not a continuous one; the base of it sloped up on the western side of the tunnel as if coming to an abrupt end. Conceivably this formed a terminal to the ditch, marking the position of an entranceway into the enclosure (and possibly corresponding with a similar causeway in the later, external ditch). Or, in common with Stonehenge and other Neolithic enclosures on chalk, it may indicate that it had been dug out in segments, a bit like a string of sausages. At other sites where segmented ditches have been recorded, the sections do not always perfectly match up, as if different groups of diggers had embarked on their task without fully planning how their portion would join with the next.

The unweathered sides of this ditch suggest that it had not been open to the elements for long before it was, very deliberately, backfilled and re-cut slightly further out. This happened not just once, but at least three times, moving

The Silbury Enclosure. The date of the enclosure is uncertain, but it is possibly earlier than the central mound.

successively outwards with each cycle of backfill and re-cut; the ditch, like ripples in water, moving ever further out. Again, the unweathered sides of these ditches suggest that re-cutting was a rapid process, a point further underlined by a dearth of snail shells. Activity was continuing at a pace, and it seems that no sooner had one ditch been dug, than it had to be filled and cut slightly further out. Perhaps the bank and ditch enclosure needed to move outwards to make room for the ever expanding chalk mound within it, or perhaps there was some

symbolism in the continuous cycle of digging, backfilling, and re-digging of ditches. Whatever the reason, the process of backfilling the ditches would have required as much material put back in them as would have ever been removed in the first place, implying that they were not just simple quarries for material, but something altogether less functional. Early Neolithic causewayed enclosure ditches frequently display such episodic backfilling and re-cutting.

After the fourth ditch had been backfilled, the Neolithic builders decided to move the ditch further out yet again, to the position in which it can be seen today and from which the chalk for the final phases of the monument was presumably quarried. The recent excavation did not cut through this prodigious external ditch; had it done so, we may have seen further ditch re-cuts, high-lighting the fact that Silbury Hill was constantly being adjusted. There was no fixed plan.

On the summit

At this point the tunnel dipped down, below the Neolithic ground level, which meant that it was no longer possible to see evidence of the later phases of the mound in the tunnel sides. Instead, an understanding of the construction of these

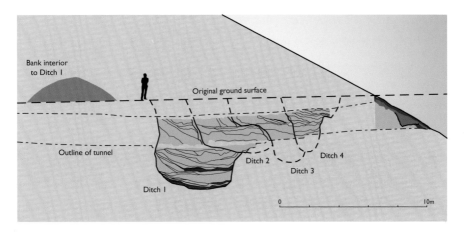

Bank interior to Ditch 1

Original ground surface

Outline of tunnel

Ditch 2

Ditch 3

Ditch 4

Ditch 1

0   10m

Section drawing showing the ditch re-cuts.

final stages comes from three small trenches that were excavated on the summit. It was a relief to leave the suffocating intensity and closeness of the tunnel; it wrapped itself around you as you entered, and the lack of an external view forced concentration on the tunnel sides, focusing only on the minutiae of the mound. On the summit it was possible to breathe deeply; to feel the wind and weather, and from this lofty perch, eye level with the hovering kestrels, to see immense distances, letting your mind soar. Or, as we did, watch crop circles being made by a group of people in a nearby field. This alone made up for the thrice-daily, and sometimes more, yomp up the steep, spiralling path to the summit.

The deposits on the top were made up of dumps of crushed chalk, laid one on top of another and held in place by large, loose pieces of chalk rubble, which effectively formed a rough revetment wall built in concentric rings. The walls were carefully tilted inwards to hold the chalk in place, thus preventing collapse. A similar technique to this was used to backfill the ditches seen in the tunnel and clearly represents the construction technique used to build the final phases of the monument. Indeed, a similar technique was recorded at the great bank at Avebury by the famous early 20th-century archaeologist Alexander Keiller, and again at the huge henge enclosure at Marden, between Avebury and Stonehenge, excavated by another prominent archaeologist, Geoff Wainwright, at the same time that Atkinson was working at Silbury.[8] A henge, it should be noted, was a bank and ditch enclosure, with the bank on the outside of the ditch thus indicating its non-defensive nature. This method of building the mound at Silbury is as ingenious as it is simple. The rubble walls hold the horizontal chalk layers in place, making it extremely stable. The voids left by the loose-fitting rubble allow rainwater to drain freely through the great mound, thereby limiting erosion. It is the reason the mound is still standing 4,500 years later.

Archaeologist Duncan Stirk photographs one of the chalk rubble walls on the summit. (661-6343-19)

As the final remnants of the topsoil and subsoil were mattocked, shovelled and scraped away from the main 3m × 5m excavation trench on the summit, the tops of these chalk revetment walls became visible. A small patch within one of the walls, however, looked distinctly different, and as excavation proceeded at its customary cautious and careful pace the reason became obvious. Rather than using chalk rubble to build the wall, this small area was made from broken pieces of sarsen rubble. Lying alongside them were pieces of picks made from red deer antler. These sarsen stones are extraordinarily heavy, certainly when compared to similarly sized chalk blocks. Having carried them down the hill, we would not recommend the task of carrying them up, and it is difficult to imagine a practical reason for using them. Further, these sarsen fragments seem to have been deliberately placed next to the antler. A closer examination of Atkinson's archive slides from his 1970 excavation revealed similar clusters of sarsen stones within the walls dotted throughout his much larger trench, and therefore this strange phenomenon seems widespread throughout the later construction phases of the mound. Indeed, one is visible eroding out of the present pathway close to the summit, while a layer of sarsen was noted in the open shaft at a depth of about 10m.

The sarsen fragments on the summit were different to those seen within the tunnel. The fragments from the summit were formed largely of broken pieces, many with flake scars indicative of the sort of knapping you might normally associate with flint – contrasting with the whole, rounded boulders recovered from inside the mound. One sarsen stone from the summit even appears to have been knapped into a rough sub-oval shape before being lightly pecked and ground, as if making a quernstone, and then, quite deliberately, split by a single blow.

The shape of Silbury

The shape of the final Neolithic Silbury is difficult to determine and requires an awful lot of guesswork as to what is original and what is a later modification. In profile the mound appears a little lop-sided, the west and north-western slopes appearing to bow out. This can readily be observed in photographs. The other sides comprise a steep but regular incline. When contours were plotted it became apparent that the mound is not in fact truly circular, but built in a series of straight lengths, and its outer shape may have been dictated by a series of radial spines, between which are straight construction lines forming something like a spider's web (*see* page 75). Whether this form occurred throughout the mound is not clear, but it could have been dictated by a series of buttresses that help tie the structure together. The number of straight sides is not absolutely clear, as much of the surface is masked by weathering, but it could be as many as nine at the base, and higher in the mound it is possible that the form changes slightly. Towards the summit it appears even more angular; on the penultimate ledge, for example, an almost right-angled change in direction can be observed, while the summit itself appears to be rectangular rather than circular. This, of course, could also be the result of later activity.

The earthworks provided some surprises. When the circumference of the uppermost and well-defined ledge was perambulated, the circuit could not be completed. Instead one arrives at a position several metres lower than the starting point; the ledge as we see it is in fact a spiral. This was in fact a feature that had been observed earlier by Alasdair Whittle.[9] Some caution is required in extending this point too far, for it is not clear now whether the spiral continued to incorporate ledges further down the mound. And again, neither is it clear from surface observation whether it was an original feature or a result of later, perhaps medieval, modification. One thing that is certain is that it does not appear to be recent, as the footpath present on Aubrey's sketch of around 1665 cuts across it,[10] and the idea that Silbury Hill was reconstructed as a garden mount or other early modern landscape feature similar to the nearby Marlborough Mount can be discounted. Nevertheless, such a spiral feature would make some sense both in terms of construction and for later access, and it is worth noting that large structures of the ancient world such as ziggurats and pyramids were built in this fashion, as were more recent large mounds such as that commemorating the Battle of Waterloo in Belgium.

In the trench on the summit there appeared to be no particular finish to the prehistoric deposits recorded, and nor were there any later stratified layers covering them; only the Neolithic mound and a disturbed soil horizon – nothing else. And although it is not something that can easily be demonstrated, one has to speculate whether this actually was the original summit. Did the chalk walls formerly continue upwards so that the mound was higher? Has the summit been lost in the years between the Neolithic and the first drawings of the Hill? If so, the original shape can only be guessed at – perhaps it was rounded.

The radiocarbon dates taken from the Hill suggest that its overall construction was rapid, thrown up in the years between 2400 and 2300 BC, and therefore it perhaps took only three or four generations to go from the small gravel mound to the massive final chalk mound. Work on it, therefore, must have been frenzied at times, perhaps punctuated by short periods when nothing occurred.

The end of the tunnel works

Archaeological work in the tunnel was completed on Friday 16 November 2007, and preparations were made to backfill the tunnel and all the voids. Before this, however, a cable was buried into the natural chalk, well below the floor of the tunnel (and therefore under, rather than in, the mound), so that electrical measurements could continue to be made after it had been backfilled. This would allow the condition of the backfill to be monitored after the tunnel was sealed and should one day, as technology improves, allow much more sophisticated geophysical imaging of the Hill's interior – a non-destructive way of seeing what else lies within. The tunnel was then backfilled using chalk that had been sourced from the same geological strata as the original chalk mound – it was mixed with water and pumped back in, although a few sandbags containing this same chalk were required around the organic mounds in the centre, in order to prevent a reaction between the acidic organics and alkaline chalk.

Where possible, the miners retrieved the mining arches; working back from the centre, they removed them as they pumped the chalk in. Around the central area, however, at the site of the 2007 collapse, a few of the arches had to be left in position, for it was simply not safe enough to remove them – ultimately these few pieces of steel have remained to become part of the Hill.

Finally, the concrete portal around the entrance to the tunnel was dismantled as the tunnelling works drew to a close. The 1968 concrete lintel and the green steel door were taken out and given to the Alexander Keiller Museum in Avebury. The rear of the concrete lintel contained a final gift: a glass bottle contained a rolled-up letter identifying all those who worked on the 1960's project. The polystyrene blocks were removed from the crater on the summit, and this too was filled in with the same chalk as the tunnel, all of which was archaeologically monitored. The work was finally finished in May 2008; a year almost to the day after it had begun. The compound was taken away piece by piece; the village grew smaller and smaller until finally all that remained was a single office chair, surreally left in the middle of the field. With the on-site works finished, the difficult task of making sense of what had been recorded could start.

6 Making sense of the mound

'The past is a foreign country: they do things differently there,' wrote L P Hartley as the opening line of the *Go-Between*. If that is the case, then the prehistoric period must surely be another world, for it is manifestly different to our own lives and perhaps lies beyond our intellectual and emotional understanding. Indeed, the more we know about it, the odder it seems to become. So, how do we make sense of the mound?

Silbury Hill has figured widely in the academic literature, often taking centre stage in grand interpretations of the period. It has been seen by some as evidence for an established chiefdom with a ranked society – Silbury providing clear evidence that those in power were able to organise a large labour force.[1] Other interpretations see the monument as the very process that created the elite, the summit forming an exclusive ceremonial arena that quite literally raised them above the common people.[2] These interpretations mostly concentrate on Silbury's sheer size; the mound reduced to passively reflecting imbalances in society.[3] Indeed, its monstrous size has engendered an almost equally monstrous amount of discussion of the amount of work involved in constructing it. There is now a bewildering array of statistics, most of which, slightly alarmingly, seem to be concerned with how much it would cost to build it anew. In the 17th century, John Aubrey claimed it would cost 'four score thousand pounds to make the hill now'. William Stukeley put it at the lower cost of £20,000 in 1743, while Edward Drax corrected him, suggesting that it would cost exactly £56,495 and 9d.[4] In 1907, in a clear case of deflation, the estimated cost once again fell to £20,000.[5] Richard Atkinson suggested that a permanent work force of 500 people would have taken 10 years to construct the mound,[6] while others suggest 1,000 people for 2 years.[7]

Alasdair Whittle considered the options comprehensively and carefully and found it difficult to imagine the monument as anything other than a symbol of spiritual belief, the summit perhaps bringing people closer to the heavens, stating that 'Perhaps we could envisage prophets shouting at the sky from the top'. Whittle considered that the mound was possibly constructed out of religious fervour, which has certainly led to other monumental works, such as Chartres cathedral. The unique quality of Silbury even led him to wonder whether someone had travelled to Egypt and seen the early pyramids or at least heard stories of their existence; 'the unusual', he reminds us, 'may require unusual explanations'.[8]

These represent a fine array of interpretations, each reflecting the academic traditions or fashions from which they emerged. However, as discussed earlier, the flat top may owe more to modifications in later periods, and therefore any interpretation involving activity on the summit or the position of the summit may be something of a red herring. This aside, there is a compelling problem regarding many interpretations in that they ignore the complex beginnings of the monument and the subsequent chronology. Those who dumped the gravel on the ground cannot possibly have known what the final manifestation of the monument would appear like or the phases that it would go through or that it would take several generations to complete. They could not have predicted precisely what could be seen from the summit as it reached any particular height.

In fact, those involved were instrumental in generating the changing form of the Hill, the way that it developed, mutated, evolved and metamorphosed from one form to another. The site started with the ground being prepared and a gravel mound piled on it, before becoming a larger stake-defined mound surrounded by smaller mounds. In the next phase pits were dug into the top of the central mound, before the whole complex became covered by a larger organic mound. The site took on an entirely different character after this when a massive ditch was dug that probably formed a circuit, 100m in diameter, with an internal bank that enclosed all this earlier activity. Not even this enclosure ditch was straightforward, though; the unweathered sides show that it had been rapidly backfilled and then re-cut a number of times. Again the mound was enlarged with chalk – but not as a single construction. Instead, it happened incrementally with a series of ring doughnut-like banks of chalk being added to the outside of it. The enclosure ditch was backfilled and a further ditch dug beyond it, leaving space for the mound to be enlarged further. Silbury, in other words, was not a single construction project but the focus for an array of activities; activities that may well have taken quite different forms. This elaborates on Atkinson's three-phased arrangement and contrasts with most interpretations of the site that focus on the final form of Silbury, as if the builders had some sort of blueprint, by-passing the drama and excitement of the development and growth of the monument and consequently the real point that lay behind it.

A different way of understanding

This is a peculiarly western way of viewing monuments, influenced by commercial perceptions of the world, and archaeological monuments are considered in a similar way to modern buildings. They are considered as if constructed to a blueprint, where their final form is pre-planned and which represents the most important aspect. The construction work is regarded simply as a process that has to followed in order to get something built. This is probably why archaeologists have often focused on calculations of cost and labour input. But one thing is certain: those who constructed Silbury would have had a different set of beliefs, values and ways of seeing the world. People from other cultures often see things rather differently.

Artificially constructed round mounds appear all over the world, from Britain and Europe, to Asia, Australia and the Americas, and are remarkably persistent across many different time periods. There are many possible examples, all slightly different, and it is worth travelling across continents and oceans of time to consider how round mounds elsewhere can be constructed. There are both archaeological and ethnographic instances and there will of course be different emphases and interpretations from place to place. One is considered here – that of the Hopewellian mounds in North America.

Making sense of the mound

The Hopewellian mounds of the Middle Woodland Period (approximately 50 BC to AD 400) provide an excellent case to study. Some of these mounds covered depressions known as ritual basins, although most covered wooden structures that may or may not contain burials. Structures were dismantled or burnt and then 'midden' debris (what we would call domestic rubbish), along with earth and other materials, was ceremonially added to form the mound.[9] The availability of historically recorded Native American myths and beliefs provides something to compare with the archaeology, and may provide us with a brief glimpse into some of the possible reasons why round mounds were constructed within this culture. Professor Robert L Hall (who has Native American ancestry) suggests in his excellent book *An Archaeology of the Soul: North American Indian Belief and Ritual* that, according to origin myths, the use of black mud and clay in the centre of many of these mounds could symbolise the mud from which the earth was formed.[10] In these myths the world was created when the Earth Diver, represented by an animal whose species varies regionally but could be anything from a muskrat to a duck, plunged to the bottom of the vast expanse of the primordial sea and brought up some mud in its paws, claws, feet or beak. Once above the water, the mud began to expand to create land. The black, peaty, waterlogged mud used to build the Hopewellian mounds can then perhaps be seen as a re-enactment of the Earth Diver myth;[11] the audience actively participating in the story as it is being retold through building the mound. To create the mound was to create the world. Similar origin myths can be found all over the planet, and variations of the Earth Diver theme can be found throughout Europe, Russia, Mongolia, ancient Egypt and across Asia, where, in the latter, the primordial boar retrieved a lump of mud from the bottom of the cosmic ocean on the end of its snout; once raised to the surface, it promptly swelled to form the primordial mound, creating land.[12]

Of course, this has nothing to do with the British Neolithic and we are not suggesting that Silbury Hill should be interpreted in exactly this way, for there is a whole spectrum of potential beliefs that might be drawn upon in support of one point of view or another. But the Hopewellian case underlines the fact that beliefs in the Neolithic are likely to have been far more complex than may be popularly assumed. People of this period were not influenced by western modern economics or values. The important point with this example is that the actual *process* of construction was as important as the final form, perhaps more so. In fact 'construction' is a misleading term, since the Hopewellian community did not build mounds so much as 'author' them;[13] the soils in the mound were designed to be read and understood in relation to the mythical stories. The final form can better be seen as a by-product of myth re-enactment, afterwards left standing as an enduring reminder – a memorial – to the mythological story. Perhaps in a similar way Silbury was also authored; the soils, important to the builders and imbued with symbolism, were placed in an ordered fashion that was designed to be read and understood – to tell a story – as they were being laid down.

Can soils really have symbolism?

By all accounts the last England football match at the old Wembley Stadium on 7 October 2000 was a drab affair; England's lacklustre performance resulting in a 1–0 loss to Germany. Hardly a worthy end to nearly three quarters of a century of glory at the stadium. But that is how it finished. The formal pilgrimage down Wembley Way to the twin towers was no more. After this, the stadium was demolished and the football pitch was cut up into small bits of turf and sold to collectors eager to have a little bit of the hallowed ground. The massive amount of rubble, clay and soil dug up during the demolition was not put into landfill as would normally happen from a less sacred site, but was turned instead into four huge conical mounds just outside London. To all outward appearance they resemble latter-day Silburys made up of the soil sanctified by decades of iconic sporting events and rock concerts.

So even here in the West, where there is a clear divide between nature and culture, soil carries meaning for us; it can be imbued with cultural characteristics. Soils can be significant, and in many cultures and traditions across the planet they form the sacred land and are saturated with symbolism.

There are plenty of examples of prehistoric monuments where the material used in their construction seems to have been specially chosen. This can be seen in the megalithic monuments of western Europe. The stones are not arranged haphazardly according to availability, expediency or practicality, but in specific patterns distinguished by the texture and colour of the stones. Some of the stones were brought from far afield, suggesting that perhaps the place of origin was an important aspect of their use. The stones, in other words, carried a message or perhaps a constellation of messages embedded within them; messages that people would have interpreted – they had meaning.[14] And it is not just the stones of megaliths that appear to have been carefully selected; the soils and turves of a number of late Neolithic and Bronze Age earthen mounds also appear to have been carefully placed, the various components ordered according to their distinctive and often contrasting colours and textures.[15]

This is also true of Silbury Hill. The material making up the mound appears to have been thoughtfully and deliberately selected, the soil making up each organic phase having come from a particular geological location. Whilst the soil used in one of the mini-mounds seems to have come from a woodland setting, it contrasts with the soil from the main mound, which had a grassland setting. These dark organic mounds all contrast starkly with the underlying yellow gravels used in the gravel mound, as well as the overlying chalk phases. Sarsen boulders were deliberately incorporated into at least two of the phases; not as a setting on top or around the base, nor indeed so that they were visible at all. Instead, they were actually placed in the body of the mound, with no discernible practical purpose. Knowledge of their existence seems to have been of paramount importance. On the summit, the large, heavy sarsen boulders were incorporated into the chalk walls. The fact that they were carried all the way up suggests a real motivation. There also seems to have been a definite association between sarsen stone and fragments of antler picks, since a cluster of picks was placed alongside the sarsens. Antler fragments were found throughout the chalk phases of the mound. Although some were small fragments easily incorporated by accident, others were really quite large, including a near-complete pick. It is difficult to see how these could have been incorporated other than through deliberate inclusion.

Perhaps the soil for the earlier phases was brought to the site by members of a local community, each bringing a basket-load of earth from their home ground. By incorporating a patch of home turf in the mound they created an enduring link with the monument; claiming or reaffirming family rights to live in the area through the creation of a communal monument; or renewing the mythic connections that bound these people to this part of the land. Partaking in the construction may have even been thought to bring luck or good health. Or perhaps like the Hopewellian mounds of North America, Silbury was formed out of literal retellings of mythical tales – acts from a different world embodied and made permanent on this one. Silbury thus became the physical embodiment of years and decades of public performances. Either way, one is left with an overwhelming sense that the creators of Silbury Hill recognised a profound symbolism in the soils, stones and other materials and used them in a highly specified way; the very act of which was designed to be read and comprehended by the community.

The ditch

The mound, however, is only part of the monument. It is worth considering the ditch, which was deliberately constructed by digging into the lower slope of the hillside and being expanded to form a rectangular area alongside. The original digging of the ditch must have been an enormous affair, and care was taken in the way that it was done. There was no need to extract material from such a great depth if it was simply to provide material for a mound, as it would have been relatively easy to quarry into the adjacent hillside. Alfred Pass's 1886 shafts (*see* Chapter 2) show that in most cases the ditch filling consisted of white clay that had been deposited by water, but close by the mound a large amount of chalk rubble was present that had evidently eroded from the mound. Significantly, within the westernmost ditch terminal was a deposit of 'many' sarsen boulders that may have fallen from the mound. Pass remarked that even in September, after a long dry summer, water stood at a depth of 2.5m in these holes, and indeed the Beckhampton stream must have found its way into the ditch and at certain times of the year made digging difficult.[16] Astonishingly in an area of absorbent chalk, the ditch and its extension retained water. Military terminology might describe it as a moat and Pass observed that the mound would have been quite defensible.

Ditches, however, carry additional significance in other parts of the world. For example, rather than for defence against their enemies, ditches might be dug in order to impede malevolent spirits and ensure that they get bogged down. Looked at like this, the perimeters of enclosures could behave like North American dream catchers, a spider's web-like embroidered device believed to filter out bad dreams. More than half a century ago Herbert Taylor pointed out that the ditch around a Bronze Age ceremonial monument at Tyning's Farm in the Mendip Hills could not have been primarily a quarry for mound material as the mound overlay it, and neither could it be an architectural feature as the mound was allowed to cover it. Being a slight affair it did not constitute an obstacle to humans. Instead he thought that it must represent some magical or religious function.[17] Perhaps he had in mind the need to keep malign spirits in or out and the possibility that they might get trapped in the ditch, as is believed to be the case with some earthworks in Africa.[18]

The ditch being dug using antler picks.

The mound, aged, weathered, eroded, and grassed over may still have attracted ceremonies centuries later.

The final development and form

It is clear from the archaeological work at Silbury Hill that it evolved and grew gradually, in a piecemeal fashion. However, at some stage in the development of the mound, particularly as it grew in size, this mutating process must have resolved into an ever more formal construction, perhaps with the original meanings and purposes lost. As the mound grew to proportions that posed serious safety risks, there must have been a necessity to provide revetment and greater solidity to the structure, and this can be seen by the chalk rubble walls that were present in at least the outer casing. The point at which this change occurred is unknown, since the greater proportion of the mound has not been investigated archaeologically.

It is not known whether it ever reached a 'final mound'; whether there was a grand unveiling of the monument; or whether, perhaps due to a shift in the nature of beliefs and ceremonial activity, it just stopped being added to. It is unlikely, however, to have been gleaming white for long, as it is so often depicted. Indeed, it is likely that within a few years of fresh chalk being added to the Hill, colonisation by plants would have started. The experimental chalk mound constructed nearby on Overton Down in 1960 showed that within the first twenty-odd years, a mosaic of broken patchy vegetation cover had formed on the sides, with smaller bare areas on the top.[19] Of course, the Hill could have been deliberately weeded to maintain its whiteness, much like the chalk figures are today. Alternatively, the chalk may have been scattered with soil and seeds to encourage re-vegetation.

Musician Simon O'Dwyer using a reproduction of the Loughnashade trumpet (from the Irish Bronze Age) on Silbury Hill.

Once the mound had reached its maximum size it continued to be used and adapted for other purposes. From the summit one would have had a clear view into the West Kennet palisaded enclosures and parts of Avebury henge. And the size of the Hill and the location of it in a natural bowl also give it good acoustic properties, which may well have been later exploited to provide 'otherworldly' aspects to the experience of ritual. With this in mind, English Heritage archaeologist Sarah May conducted an experiment in 2007 into the Hill's acoustic properties: she asked musicians to play instruments from the summit, such as stone whistles, frame drums, bone flutes, wooden flutes ('Wicklow pipes'), animal horns and bronze horns, and used volunteers placed throughout the area to record what they could hear; the results were then digitally modelled. The volunteers reported how clear the sound transmission was. It was particularly good to the south, towards the Swallowhead spring, but less obvious towards Avebury to the north.

The final mound may have been viewed in many different ways, informing or commemorating the local traditions, mythologies and cosmologies. Whereas the earlier phases of activity may have been no more than occurred elsewhere in Britain, the chalk structure at that time did not exceed the size of other

Newgrange in the Boyne Valley, Ireland. The massive mound with ornamental facade and peristalith of carved stones covers a stone-lined passage tomb.

Neolithic mounds such as Newgrange in Ireland, the 7-metre high Maes Howe in the Orkneys, or the 12-metre high La Hougue Bie on Jersey. The later stage of Silbury Hill was different – reaching a massive 31m, the activities were unique and made the site truly monumental. A brief look at other monumental mounds across the world shows the variety of interpretations involved. The pyramids of Egypt have already been alluded to as have, in passing, the ziggurats of the Middle East. In North America, a Silbury Hill-shaped mound, surrounded by a wide ditch with a single causeway, was constructed in stages over about a century from about 250 BC at Grave Creek, West Virginia, adjacent to the Ohio River. The final construction reached 21m in height. With a nod in the direction of past and future antiquarian activities at Silbury, a shaft was sunk from the

The temple mound, Mound A, one of three square mounds at Etowah, Georgia, United States. One of the smaller mounds can be seen to the left.

summit and a horizontal tunnel dug from the perimeter in 1838. Later mounds of the Mississippian Culture constructed between 1000 and 1500 AD achieved even greater monumentality. The unusual bird-shaped Mound A at Poverty Point, Louisiana, with a ramp leading to the summit, reaches some 21m in height and is thought to have been constructed over a relatively short time span. One of three square mounds alongside the river at Etowah near Cartersville, Georgia, reached 19m in height. None of these mounds approaches the height of Silbury, but their basal area can be larger and the amount of material shifted just as great. Emerald Mound, near Natchez, Mississippi, is just 10m high but covers an area of some 3 hectares. However, upon it are two further mounds that provide a total height of over 19m. The largest, Monk's Mound at Cahokia, formed of four terraces or levels, is 30.5m high with a base of 305m measured north–south and 236m east–west. All of these appear to have been constructed in stages and appear in groups of three or four. At Cahokia, there is a group of 120 mounds. Some had buildings on the summit and are referred to as Temple Mounds, while others contained burials and are considered to be funeral mounds. Some were formed as successive buildings were constructed and burnt or dismantled and others built on top.[20] In some cases, historical accounts supplement archaeological observations. At the Natchez Village site, for example, this was true of the Great Sun Mound, where a sequence of low earthen platforms each containing a building was constructed over the last. The building was a ritual centre occupied by the tribal chief. An adjacent mound, Temple Mound, supported a temple building.[21] Festivities and ceremonies took place at regular agricultural and subsistence-based occasions within a 13-month, lunar calendar.

In Europe, monumental mounds occur in Brittany, particularly around Carnac where the massive prehistoric tumulus of Saint-Michel reaches 12m in height and, like La Hougue Bie, has a chapel on the summit. These invariably cover earlier features and are formed in stages. Saint-Michel, however, is a long mound and round mounds in the area are of lesser dimensions. The massive 16-metre high mound of Krakus looms large over the city of Krakow in Poland. Thought to date to the 10th century AD and half the size of Silbury, it was excavated in the 1930s. It was constructed around a central post with seven radial fence lines separating nine different segmented deposits [22]. It is worth recalling the straight sides recorded at Silbury and whether they might represent similar construction elements. There are other ethnographic examples that suggest such figures might be of importance. Four thousand miles away in the United States, a series of spoked monuments without covering mounds exist. One of the best known, the Medicine Wheel at Bighorn, Wyoming, has 28 spokes, a number thought to represent the lunar cycle, the symbolism of which is retained in the rafters of ceremonial lodges. Here too there is thought to have originally been a central post. Four thousand miles away in the opposite direction, the Chakra or wheel is neatly emblazoned on the flag of India, a 24-spoke spinning wheel version of the ancient 8-spoked chariot or Dharma wheel. The overall shape, a circle, is thought to represent perfection, while each spoke represents a virtue such as kindness, justice, love, courage and patience.[23]

Around the world there are beliefs that the circle is a sacred form, that it represents the passage of human life, the cycle of the year, month and day, of the sun and moon and of the cosmos; or in the natural world of ripples in water, or the shape of nests and beaver lodges. A circle has no end; to the Native Americans it symbolises life – for example, the seven sacred circles of the Lakota encapsulate life and its key ceremonies. Five thousand miles away, the enormous spiritual complex known as the Temple of Heaven in Beijing reflects the ancient Chinese belief that heaven is round and the earth is square. Set within an outer wall 6.5km in length and aligned to the points of compass, it encloses 273 hectares and was a sacred place where the wishes of people were conveyed to heaven. Sacrificial activities took place at the winter solstice and at the summer solstice, asking for rain, while Ming and Qing dynasty emperors prayed for a good harvest. Its position in the countryside is instructive. Like Silbury it was deliberately constructed on a slope. Within the complex, the northern end is higher and considered closer to heaven, while the southern is lower and closer to the earth. The northern part of the outer wall is semicircular to reflect the dome of heaven, while the southern is square to reflect the flat earth. Internally, circular structures reflect heaven and square ones the earth.[24]

Back to Silbury

This provides but a glimpse at the range of ways of interpreting mounds and circular monuments, but after this breathtaking journey around the world it is time to come back to Wiltshire. So far this discussion has focused very much on the mound itself, but to really understand Silbury we need to stand on the summit and look out at the broader surroundings; for this monument simply cannot be disconnected from the other monuments or the countryside in which it was created. For that reason the next chapter will discuss the setting of Silbury and how it fits in with the other monuments and the broader British Neolithic.

7 Land, stones and the development of monuments

Rendered into countless photographs and paintings, the open land around Silbury, with its isolated nests of trees and patchwork of pasture and cultivated fields, is today considered attractive, aesthetic and picturesque; the epitome of English countryside. This perfect and ideal vision of the land as a visual canvas results from the ability to pass through it as an objective observer in order to acknowledge the panorama. All that is needed is a frame. The very name 'landscape' derives from *landschap*, a Dutch school of painting dating from the 16th century. In transforming the land to a 'scape', however, it is anaesthetised and stripped of its character; the character that would have been recognised by its occupants in times past.

Those living on the land have a different perception. The land can be dirty, cold, wet and smelly. There are warm parts and cold parts; welcome and unwelcome. There are nooks and crannies that provide shelter from the elements and others that are uncomfortable to be in. All parts of the land have their characteristics, and they will have been as well known to the inhabitants as are our living rooms to us. Undoubtedly they will have had names, perhaps reflecting the nature of their aspect, distinctive vegetation, or relating to events that occurred there. Parts of the land may also have been considered a little like the French *terroir*, where particularly warm, sheltered, easily cultivated soils conspired to produce areas valued for cultivation or settlement. The Vikings divided their settlements and land according to the path of the sun, so that each individual had a fair amount of 'sun' land and 'shadow' land, that is to say, land that received the low winter sun early in the day and land that did not. Even today gardeners relish south-facing gardens, and we can be in no doubt that the value of such plots of land will have been observed early in prehistory.

Exactly how prehistoric individuals perceived this land is difficult to know, for the vegetation and along with it the fauna has changed considerably, but so have beliefs and expectations. It is certain that prehistoric people will not have shared our economic or commercial values, or our religious ones. And their antennae will no doubt have placed a greater reliance on senses other than the visual, those of sound, smell and taste. But the world was not flat. The dramatic hills and escarpments of the Wiltshire chalk made it possible to look down on land from certain vantage points and visualise it in map form. It was possible to stand and watch the buzzards soaring alongside before they captured the movement of an unfortunate mouse in the valley below and descended to settle on it. But accessing the currents of air was another matter completely. The wind was unexplained, sometimes warm and sometimes cold, and without knowledge of meteorology, only supernatural explanations could be entertained. The sky formed such a major component of the world, yet it was impossible to investigate it, and the clouds and celestial figures – the sun, moon and stars – all remained objects beyond rational comprehension.

Land of stones

The form of the land around the monument was largely dictated by processes related to the last Ice Age. The ice sheet itself did not reach this far south, but for extensive periods the land would have been covered in deep snow. For millennia the frozen ground was subject to summer thawing before being re-frozen during the winter months. Meltwater, impeded by flint seams and frozen chalk, erupted from valley sides and assisted the process of solifluction whereby huge quantities of soluble chalk and flint were washed from the higher ground to be deposited further down valleys and coombes. The southerly course of the sun around the sky resulted in the formation of lop-sided valleys, as east-facing slopes received warmth earlier in the day and melted at a quicker rate than the other. Coombes and valleys already scoured by earlier freeze and melt processes were enhanced

A group of sarsen boulders on Overton Down, Wiltshire, remnants of a much larger accumulation.

and made deeper, while new ones were established. Layers of disturbed flint were washed from their deposits in the parent chalk, down the valley sides to rest on the valley floor between Devizes and Beckhampton and along the River Kennet, while water, trapped where landslides and soliflucted material collected, may have formed small lakes.

But this was also a land of stones. Sarsen, a silicified sandstone that millions of years previously had formed a crust on the land, was broken up and, under gravity, massive boulders edged into valleys and coombes. In some places they were so thickly strewn across the land surface that it was possible to step from one to another for great distances without touching the ground, in places with one on top of another. Millennia later, Samuel Pepys, Daniel Defoe, Osborne White and others gazed in astonishment at these sarsens, or 'grey wethers' as Aubrey had called them, on account of the fact that from a distance they looked like grazing sheep. Aubrey thought that the area resembled a scene where giants had used rocks in a fight with the gods. Since Pepys's day they have been largely removed for building and road construction, and more recently the process of removal has been assisted by government grants in clearing land. Groups of sarsen still lie in old ponds or hedgerows where they have been hauled by tractors, or have been sold in garden centres for use in rockeries. An indication of their former extent, however, can be obtained from a glance at early large-scale Ordnance Survey maps or the maps published by the Reverend A C Smith in 1884 after his investigation of local monuments.[1]

Peopling this land

When the turf was first cut away on the edge of the chalk bluff that was to become Silbury, it was not within an empty land bereft of people, but one that was already heavily engraved with the

evidence of human activity and which echoed with the footsteps of ancestors.
Long before monument construction had begun hunter-gatherer communities
lived in the Upper Kennet valley, hunting boar, deer and other wild animals in
the surrounding woodlands and using plants for food, for medicine and for a
multitude of other things.[2] They flaked nodules from the local eroding flint seams
to form their distinctive tools, and today the odd small flint flake characteristic of
this Mesolithic period (which began with the end of the last Ice Age around 9500
BC until about 4000 BC) is found here and there, providing the evidence that
these people moved through the area.

How these early inhabitants of the valley perceived the large sarsen boulders
when they encountered them is unknown, but given their rarity in the lowlands
of southern England it would be surprising if they were interpreted in an
entirely practical way.[3] Ethnographic accounts from parts of Russia describe
how stone is often considered sacred and forms the basis of sacrificial rites. In
Madagascar stone is considered a route towards achieving immortality; in South
America it forms part of origin myths and a relationship with the supernatural.

Land, stones and monuments

In North America stone objects can be perceived as being alive; in Australia stones and minerals are often considered as parts of the ancestral beings from the Dreamtime. Stone used for making tools is, in particular, widely considered sacred, having derived from the earth and containing properties and supporting traditions and myths regarding supernatural origins. The massive boulders strewn along the valleys of the Marlborough Downs may each, therefore, have been considered to have a supernatural significance.

The valley itself funnelled movement and provided a natural routeway, the river being accessed by both animals and humans for sustenance. Animals will always find a convenient route through obstacles and here, around Avebury, they will have not only engaged with the vegetation but also negotiated the boulders. The paths and trampled routes thus created will have provided a template for later activities in the land and a convenient means of negotiating the valley.

Animals, such as deer and wild cattle, will have been the first to influence the new environment and may have ensured the presence of a patchy, but shifting, mosaic of open ground during the period that archaeologists term the earlier Mesolithic. Sooner or later, however, the human population became sufficiently numerous to provide its own influence on tree and plant growth. Constant monitoring of this vegetation to ensure an annual supply of roots, fruits and hazelnuts, and then harvesting it, may have formed part of a process that in time led to small-scale cultivation.

Early Neolithic activities

Evidence of early ground preparation near Silbury Hill was found at South Street, 1km to the north-west. There, excavations beneath an earthen long barrow revealed the presence of ard marks[4] thought to have been made in the 4th millennium BC, in the earlier Neolithic period. As if to emphasise the point, a fragment of what appears to have been a flint sickle was encountered, with silica lustre along its cutting edge, the result of harvesting grasses. This episode, however, is likely to represent only small-scale cultivation, and subsistence appears to have depended to a considerable degree on stock, principally cattle herding. Not until much later (as late as the Middle

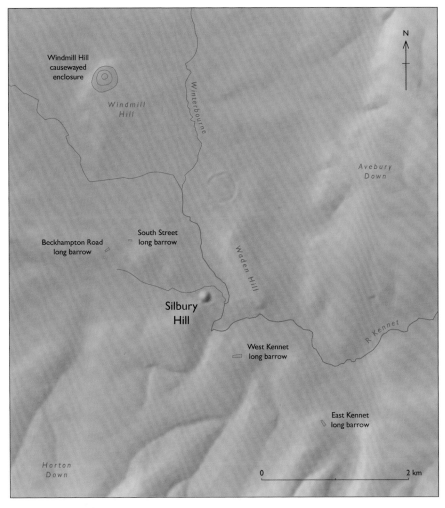

A map showing some of the early Neolithic monuments around the Silbury area.

Bronze Age around 1500 BC) did agriculture have a significant impact on the environment, with distinctive farming settlements and formalised fields. Nevertheless, initially, sarsen boulders would have been encountered even in small areas of cultivated land, and would have required removal. Given ethnographic accounts from elsewhere of ultimate respect for the natural world, intervening with nature in this way may have had its problems, and shifting such boulders might have involved appeasing supernatural elements and was perhaps done with some ceremony. It is not surprising that South Street later became the location of a long barrow.

A number of long barrows occur in the area around Silbury, and several have been excavated. These long earthen structures are sometimes associated with burial, but, like churches, they represent a number of functions over a long time span, during which any one role may have become obscured. They encapsulated ceremony, but perhaps related more to the land and its fecundity. One of the earliest occurrences at the site of the Beckhampton Road long barrow was the placing of a deposit of three ox skulls on the old ground surface, while three further ox skulls were deliberately incorporated at intervals along the length of the mound. Sometimes human bone was incorporated, although this was not

always the case. No human remains were recovered from the South Street, Horslip or Beckhampton Road barrows. But to the south of Silbury Hill lies the well-known West Kennet long barrow, where, in contrast, the bones of at least 33 individuals were found within a series of stone-built chambers, all interred within a relatively short time span.[5]

Little is known about the extremely long mound of West Kennet, but the sarsen chambers at the east end were extensively investigated by Stuart Piggott during the 1950s. Here massive boulders were set upright to form a passage with small cells leading from it and then covered over with roofing slabs. The gaps between the sarsens were infilled with drystone walls using oolitic limestone, the nearest source of which is at Calne, 10km to the west. Whether the catalyst for construction was clearance for cultivation is not clear, but the builders may have been influenced as much by natural configurations of sarsen, as by ideas from elsewhere.

One of the earliest monuments in the area is on Windmill Hill to the north-east of Silbury Hill; an early Neolithic causewayed enclosure constructed in the years before 3500 BC by the earliest farmers in the region.[6] It was created by digging three concentric circuits of interrupted ditches and throwing the spoil up to form corresponding earthen banks. The enclosure was used as a ceremonial arena or meeting place, and perhaps provided a setting for a diverse set of events and roles for the community, from exchange and feasting to the setting up of marriage alliances.

Again, not much is known of contemporary domestic settlement or what form it took, and so it is necessary to rely on the great number of flaked stone tool assemblages found in the local fields to indicate the intensity of activity. The incidence of chance discoveries of artefacts of this period, particularly of flaked and ground stone axes in the area, points to the importance of the river valleys in this regard, but besides a cluster of finds at Aldbourne some distance to the north-east, the concentration of material in the Avebury area stands out quite markedly. Whether these tools were used in an everyday domestic context, or related to the process of constructing one or other of the many local monuments, is unknown.

Of particular interest is the recovery of an enormous quantity of flint arrowheads from the slopes to the south of Windmill Hill, collected over the years from the surface. Whether these reflect activities that were associated with the causewayed enclosure or something quite different is difficult to say. It is not unknown for Neolithic enclosures elsewhere to have been attacked with arrows; Carn Brea in Cornwall and Crickley Hill in the Cotswolds both experienced that fate. The arrowheads at Windmill Hill are, however, of different ages, and so if these represent violence it must have been on a number of separate occasions. Whatever this activity was, it was one that endured, or at least recurred intermittently.

Later Neolithic activities

By the time that work on Silbury Hill had started, in the later Neolithic period, the long barrows and the enclosure on Windmill Hill were over 1,000 years old. Consequently, the area was already saturated with evidence of past use; it was a place that was heavily inscribed with folk memories that recalled ancestors and their origins.

The later Neolithic period saw a second burst of major monument construction. Two simple enclosures were built, one to the north-west between Beckhampton and Avebury (the Longstones Enclosure), and a second at Avebury itself. In addition, the already ancient Windmill Hill causewayed enclosure witnessed re-use. The Longstones Enclosure, an oval ditch 110m × 140m, dates to sometime between 2820 and 2660 BC,[7] while an enclosure at Avebury

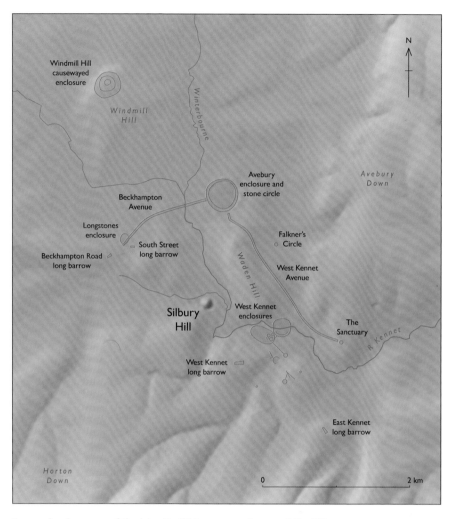

A map showing some of the later Neolithic monuments around the Silbury area.

may date to the earlier part of that time. Little is known about the latter as the massive henge that we see today was constructed on top of it, probably a little before 2500 BC.[8] This is an enormous monument, 400m in diameter that encloses some 11.5 hectares. It is bounded by a deep, wide ditch where the spoil has been placed externally to form a bank that still reaches 3m in height, this being revetted with chalk block walls similar to those at Silbury Hill.

On the floodplain of the stream and surrounding banks at West Kennett, two similar oval enclosures were formed. Unlike the others, the perimeters were marked by a palisade of enormous posts rather than ditches, and in some places lines of posts led off from the enclosures, antennae-like, to link them with smaller circular sub-enclosures.[9] The posts were massive, some the size of telegraph poles, and they as a whole required a vast amount of timber. Remarkably, these enclosures incorporated the stream within their boundaries. Distinctive Grooved Ware pottery was recovered during the excavations, and radiocarbon dates place their construction between 2500 and 2000 BC.

Locally, the interest in stones resurfaced, and during the latter half of the 3rd millennium BC the vast sarsen monoliths that formed the outer stone circle at the great henge at Avebury were erected, as may have been two parallel rows of stone monoliths known as the Beckhampton Avenue that led from Avebury westwards to Beckhampton. Although these remain undated, they are thought to date to soon after 2500 BC when the Longstones Enclosure was demolished to make way for the Avenue.[10] A similar date might be considered for the partially reconstructed West Kennet Avenue that can be traced from the southern entrance to the Avebury Henge towards the River Kennet. Following Stukeley's interpretation, the West Kennet Avenue is usually thought to have extended as far as the Sanctuary, which was a group of circular concentric settings of both wooden posts and stone monoliths on the spur of Overton Hill, 2km to the east of Silbury Hill. The purpose of these impressive avenues of stone is unknown, but perhaps they marked pathways that had mythical or some other significance: perhaps they linked important points in the land. The popular view is that processions of people journeyed down them, from one ceremonial arena to the next, the avenues

An edge-ground flint chisel from Silbury Meadow. Length 70mm. (Courtesy Alexander Keiller Museum, Avebury. DP100095)

A broken ripple-flaked oblique flint arrowhead found in Silbury Meadow. These delicate pieces are often found in Yorkshire and are also present at the large henge monuments in southern Britain. Two others were found nearby at the West Kennet palisaded enclosures. (Courtesy Alexander Keiller Museum, Avebury. DP100094)

providing real and tangible evidence that the monuments were considered as an integrated whole. Equally, it could be that the stones monumentalised something that was there before and may have been taboo and thus had to be avoided, or else represented the routes taken by supernatural beings. Some evidence suggests that many of these stone settings at and around Avebury were re-set around 2000 BC, suggesting that they, like Silbury and many prehistoric monuments, were constantly adjusted, tweaked, realigned, and reworked.

Other monuments were established around this time, but their detail need not concern us, for what is clear from this swift perambulation around the countryside is that a considerable amount of activity was taking place in the area during the years 2500 BC to 2000 BC; construction work that involved hundreds of people. The task was enormous, and a huge investment in time and labour must have been made by the local community. At times the whole Avebury area must have been a hive of activity. Silbury Hill was at the very heart of this, and it is likely that the fragile land surface around the mound still exhibits clues regarding these activities, awaiting discovery by future archaeologists. A fine but broken oblique ripple-flaked arrowhead, a type present at contemporary henge enclosures, was, for example, found adjacent to the mound in Silbury Meadow, as was a flint chisel with a ground edge, which hints at the presence of undiscovered prehistoric remains there.

New ideas and a new cultural stimulus

What initiated this intense activity is unclear, but the end of the 3rd millennium BC corresponds with the widespread introduction, into southern Britain at least, of influences from elsewhere in Europe. This is characterised, from about

2400 BC, with the introduction of the first metal: artefacts made of gold and subsequently copper, and by a new type of small, fine and beautifully decorated pottery vessel known as a Beaker. We also find a new and distinctive style of burial at this time; they are individual rather than communal, and usually accompanied by one or more Beaker vessels, as well as other grave goods, notably weapons and archery equipment. This seems to have been introduced from, or at least heavily influenced by, European traditions, and the evidence from some Beaker burials, such as the 'Amesbury Archer' near Stonehenge, suggests that some people were coming to Britain directly from the Continent (in the case of the 'Amesbury Archer', possibly from the Swiss Alps), bringing with them not only exotic artefacts and metalworking skills but new ways of thinking about the world. Metalworkers may have been considered to have supernatural powers with the production of metal seen as a magical process; indeed, there are some ethnographic accounts that link it with fertility.[11] Individuals who travelled from the Continent may have been regarded with considerable awe and indeed there may have been linguistic barriers.[12] This period appears to be defined by the rapid spread of new ideas and must have been one of profound change, representing a considerable shift in belief systems and technologies from that of earlier periods. This is the social background in which Silbury was constructed.

So little of the chronology and detail of this period are actually understood that it is difficult to make sense of what it means for the monuments. What was Silbury's role in this process of integration and the assimilation of new ideas? Was Silbury (and the other great monuments of the later 3rd millennium) constructed by immigrants who wanted to make their mark on the indigenous population? Or does it represent a response by the existing population to these new ideas? Should we even characterise this complex picture in these simplistic terms (which may simply be a reflection of modern concerns about immigration rather than anything relevant to the Neolithic)?

Two tiny sherds of late Beaker pottery were discovered on the summit of Silbury Hill during the recent excavations. Similar fragments have been recovered from the later phases of other Neolithic monuments in the area. What are we to make of these? Can we say, on the strength of a small sherd in a late context, that

A Beaker pot from Beckhampton that accompanied the skeleton of a child of about 5 years whose grave was almost covered by a sarsen stone. Height 140mm. (Courtesy Alexander Keiller Museum, Avebury. DP100102)

Silbury is a 'Beaker monument'? Did the mound herald a new order? Or does this represent the struggle for legitimacy – a Beaker attempt to authenticate their own culture in the eyes of the indigenous population by adopting and adapting an important ancestral and sacred location; one that was already enshrined in mythology and cosmology? Or should we see it as evidence of continuity – the same people doing the same things to the same monument; the style of pottery simply changing over time? These questions cannot be answered satisfactorily. But for now it is worth re-emphasising that later Neolithic monuments develop organically, evolving with each phase, rather than to any plan, and as such perhaps they should not be characterised by a particular group, culture or ceramic tradition. The monuments, much like cultural attitudes and ideals, are forever evolving, and to fix them with a label is missing the point.

Silbury Hill and the wider world

The Avebury area was not the only place to see such monumentality during the later Neolithic. It was happening all over the country, from Land's End to the Northern Isles, although the detail varies greatly and there is huge diversity between regions in both architecture and precise timings. South of the Avebury area, on the southern part of the Salisbury Plain, a simple, almost circular enclosure was created around 3000 BC. It was a little over 100m in diameter and defined by a ditch dug into the chalk, with spoil placed to form internal and external banks. It may have had uprights, possibly Preseli 'bluestones', erected on the inside of the ditch.[13] This became what we now know as Stonehenge. Some 500 years later, the stones were removed and reset in the centre of this arena, and megaliths of sarsen were added and then rearranged. Just as with the Avebury monuments, this enclosure was surrounded by earlier monuments, including the causewayed enclosure at Robin Hood's Ball and two cursus monuments (long, parallel lengths of ditch and bank). As Stonehenge was being created, added to and re-styled, a plethora of other monuments was also being created in the same area, such as the Coneybury henge, which surrounded a pit placed there a millennium earlier, the circular timber structure of Woodhenge, and the huge henge enclosure at Durrington Walls. An earthwork avenue was constructed that linked Stonehenge with the River Avon. Together these formed an impressive complex of monuments.

A barbed and tanged arrowhead found in the topsoil on the northern slope of Silbury Hill during Atkinson's excavations. The type is characteristic of the Early Bronze Age and indicates that the mound had achieved its maximum dimensions by that date. (Courtesy Alexander Keiller Museum, Avebury. DP100103)

Set almost equidistant between Stonehenge and Silbury Hill is a further, little-known complex, focusing on the Hatfield earthworks at Marden in the Vale of Pewsey. A huge mound, said to be second only in size to Silbury Hill, once existed close to a stream, part of the headwaters of the River Avon, but was deliberately levelled for cultivation some time before 1821.[14] Nearby is a second circular monument, a small henge with dramatic earthen bank and internal ditch. These monuments at Marden are contained within the largest henge enclosure in the country, comprising a massive bank with internal ditch that cuts off a spur and links the site with the stream. Nearby is a smaller henge and two clusters of now almost levelled round barrows.

A similar complex developed further south at Dorchester in Dorset, which included (amongst others) a henge at Maumbury Rings, the Dorchester Palisade, a circular earthwork enclosure known as the Flagstones Enclosure, with a diameter around 100m, similar to that of Stonehenge, and a large henge enclosure at Mount Pleasant. The latter may have incorporated a large barrow known as the Conquer Barrow. This complex was also set amongst the remains of earlier monuments.

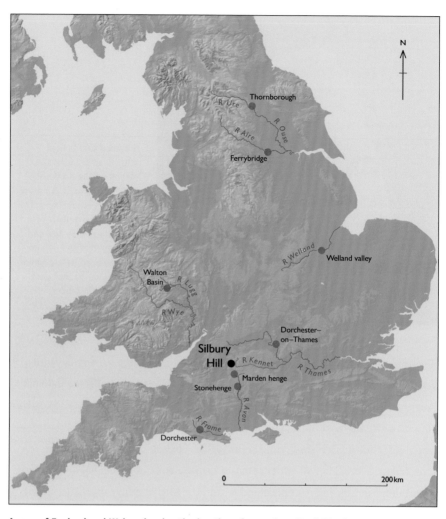

A map of England and Wales showing the location of some later Neolithic sites.

Other construction complexes occurred at Dorchester-on-Thames and elsewhere alongside the River Thames, in an area that had, again, already seen much activity. Monument complexes also developed further afield: in the Welland Valley in Cambridgeshire; the Walton basin on the Powys/Herefordshire border; at Ferrybridge and a little further north at Thornborough in North Yorkshire; Milfield in Northumberland; and further north still, in the Orkneys. Each one was set in a land that had already seen a considerable amount of activity; an ancestral land, and each located adjacent to a river or to the sea.

Monuments and water

As with Silbury, none of the individual monuments within these complexes can be understood in isolation; they are interlinked (in some cases quite literally so with the insertion of avenues between monuments) and part of the same ceremonial land. The position of these monuments near to rivers emphasises the importance of water, both in a practical way as being crucial to subsistence and movement, but also in a metaphorical and metaphysical sense. The life-giving element of water was likely to have had spiritual facets, just as it does now. Rivers play a central role in many religious traditions; perhaps the best-known example being the River Ganges, considered sacred by Hindu worshippers.

In the wide meanders of the River Thames in West London, large numbers of Neolithic ground stone axes (and later bronze artefacts) were deposited. There are clusters of such artefacts at intervals along the river, but they increase in West London. Why is not clear; perhaps it was a way of appeasing river spirits. The river provides an axis in the land,[15] a backstop, orientation; it creates a boundary; is a travel route; and has a beginning and end. It also has character which changes from youthful, bright and bubbly to laborious and sluggish with maturity. Its banks and valleys channel movement and create paths, terrestrial and riverine, which emphasise the notion of a journey, either in a metaphorical sense (the flow of the river representing a passage) or more literally with people journeying along the river by boat to the monuments. At Stonehenge, there was even an avenue linking the henge to the river. This blurs the boundaries between the river and the monuments; between what is natural and what is cultural. And so, just as the monuments are irrevocably linked to one another, so too are the monuments with the surrounding land.

This seems a good point to return to Silbury Hill, for here one cannot escape the fact that it was established close to the source of a river. In fact the rivers and the springs dominate the immediate land. To the west and east are seasonal winterbourne streams and to the south-east is the Swallowhead spring, which traditionally represents the source of the River Kennet. Pass's excavations into the ditch point to the presence of further springs within it. The low-lying position of the monument and the fact that it is surrounded by high terrain preclude the desire for height and visibility as the main reason for construction. It was not meant to be a prominent feature within the area; in fact it is relatively hidden when viewed away from its immediate environs. Instead, it is clearly associated with water, just as so many other later Neolithic monuments are.

Indeed, in such a low-lying and watery setting the huge external ditch may well have been filled with standing water for much of the year, reflecting the inverted image of the mound. The sub-rectangular extension to the ditch incorporates the Beckhampton winterbourne and may have been deliberately constructed to contain water, or perhaps to emphasise the springs: a monumentalised springhead. The water in the surrounding ditch would have acted like a mirror, reflecting the sky and the final stage mound and presenting the viewer with an image of a monument either floating in the sky or else the inverted image of the mound disappearing into the underworld.

The water may have had cosmological significance and represented a potent metaphor for movement and journeying.[16] The River Kennet flows into the River Thames around Reading. The River Thames continues the same line eastwards (towards the rising sun) and eventually flows out into the North Sea. It may be that Silbury and the rest of the Avebury complex, positioned right at the source of the River Kennet, was the start of this journey, or, for that matter, at the end of it.

Growing old

Just as the later Neolithic monumental complexes were created within ancestral landscapes, so too did these monuments age and in turn enter the realms of memory and tradition. Although the dynamism and energy that had once been harnessed to create these monuments dissipated or moved on in different directions, they were never forgotten. Throughout the following millennia, well into the historic period, Silbury continued to be used and adapted for new purposes; its meaning changing with each generation.

Silbury Hill reflected in the water-filled ditch. (DP057662)

8 From Small Town to Sele-burh

Huddled around a laptop in the Castle and Ball at Marlborough in October 2006, the geophysics team (brothers Paul and Neil Linford, Louise Martin and Andy Payne) watched as their day's work was downloaded. All day they had been laboriously dragging their caesium magnetometer cart (a strange Heath Robinson contraption on giant wheels that looks more like an entry in a village soap box derby than a piece of high-tech equipment) across the field directly south of Silbury. The caesium magnetometer is used to measure subtle variations in the magnetic field beneath the ground surface, a little like an X-ray through the soil, and is non-destructive (it is, incidentally, a common piece of kit on spacecraft used to explore the geology of planets). They had hoped to establish the line of the Roman road (the route of which is broadly followed by the modern A4) along with any roadside activity. Using a grid that ran parallel to the road, the team had managed to survey a narrow strip alongside the A4. But morale had been low all day; mainly because they felt that surveying this most northerly strip of the field was a pointless task since a large steel pipeline is laid across it and was likely to affect their results. The team were further dispirited as this bit of the field is the steepest, and their cart is a heavy piece of equipment and not easy to pull up a slope, particularly in claggy, cultivated soil – even with its giant comedy wheels. But still they trudged on, and by the end of the day a small strip of land immediately south of the road had been surveyed. Results are not immediate with a caesium magnetometer. All that can be seen at the time is a series of numbers representing the raw data. It is not until this is downloaded on to a computer and processed that an image of the surveyed area appears.

Louise Martin (left) and Paul Linford (right) from the English Heritage geophysics team surveying with their caesium magnetometer cart.

A grand discovery

Slowly, as the software ground out the results, a remarkable image began to materialise on the laptop screen, and the team leaned closer. As they expected, the presence of the steel pipe, evident as a large, linear black-and-white chequered anomaly, had wiped out much of their results, but it had not destroyed all of them. As they peered closer they could just see what looked like ditches appearing to emerge from under the pipe-disturbed area and leading south, perpendicular to the road. And then as their eyes scanned across the image, the black outline of a rectangular feature became evident: could this be the stone foundations of a building? Buoyed up by this evidence, the team went back the following day and surveyed another strip – the results were even better. All week they dragged their cart across the field, working their way southwards, surveying one strip at a time, and each evening they downloaded the data, watching, day by day, as the ditches gradually resolved themselves into enclosures and compounds, as roads developed, and as two further, larger buildings began to appear. They surveyed the field south as far as the Swallowhead spring, at which point the features seemed to peter out. The roads, the enclosures, the buildings – the evidence was clear and incontrovertible. There had been, surrounding Silbury Hill, a very large Roman settlement indeed. The team were astonished; after all, how many other people can claim to have revealed a whole settlement as spectacularly as this? It is almost impossible to believe that where these quiet fields now lie, disturbed only by the A4 traffic, a noisy and bustling small town once stood; entire lives lived out in a settlement that no longer exists. Over the following 12 months the team returned on several occasions to survey the surrounding fields, and they traced more of this settlement, but nothing quite matched the excitement of that initial discovery.

The antiquarians and the Romans

This was a significant discovery, but with hindsight perhaps not surprising. The survey was undertaken in the full knowledge that a significant amount of Romano-British activity had already been recorded in the fields around the Hill. Much of this early attention had, however, been focused on charting the course of the Roman road, which ran from *Londinium* (London), through the Roman town of *Cunetio* (today known as Mildenhall, locally pronounced My-nal) on to *Verlucio* (Sandy Lane), and from there to one of the most important religious sites in Roman Britain: *Aquae Sulis* (Bath).

Stukeley had recorded the presence of Roman coins from the summit of Silbury Hill.[1] In October 1867, working on behalf of the Wiltshire Archaeological and Natural History Society, John Wilkinson cut into the east side of the mound in search of the Roman road, which was considered by Fergusson to underlie it (*see* Chapter 2). As part of this same exercise, Wilkinson excavated a platform on which was a pile of wood ashes associated with Roman artefacts. Excavations by the Reverend A C Smith east of Silbury and north of the road uncovered a large pit, 2.5m × 3.5m that contained a variety of Roman artefacts. There were bronze coins (one of Valentinian I, AD 364–375, and another of Constans I, probably dating to between AD 340 and 350), an iron stylus, part of a pair of shears, potsherds from over 80 pots 'of ordinary type', as well as some finer wares, oyster shells, animal bones, a fragment of human bone and fragments of stone and tile. The content of this pit was summed up as 'little better than rubbish', which it may have been, but it was important rubbish and Wilkinson acknowledged in 1869 that this evidence proves 'that some Roman dwelling place must have for some time existed in the immediate neighbourhood'.[2] When Alfred Pass excavated his small trenches in 1886, he also found Roman material in the ditch extension, including a coin close to the base of the mound which was covered by 2m of ditch silt.[3] William and Henry Cunnington, leading authorities of the Wiltshire Archaeological and Natural History Society, partly excavated a Roman well in 1882. This was situated immediately south of the mound and Roman road.[4]

A little later, Mr Arnold, the tenant farmer of the field lying to the south of Silbury, noticed that no matter how many cartloads of refuse he poured on to a particular spot in his field, the land always seemed to subside. This was immediately south of the highway and south-south-east of Silbury Hill, on the lip of the bluff overlooking the floodplain. Guessing that he had probably found the location of a disused well, the perceptive farmer allowed Joshua Brooke and Benjamin Howard Cunnington to excavate, which they did in 1896.[5] Brooke was a surveyor and architect employed by the District Highways Department at Marlborough and an avid collector of antiquities; he had even developed his own museum in his house at Marlborough. His work will have ensured his familiarity with roadside 'anomalies'. With the farmer as a willing assistant, they dug down into the area of subsidence, and by the end of the first day had confirmed that it was indeed a well. Its final depth was an impressive 8.5m. It contained Romano-British material, including pottery fragments, animal bones, oyster shells, a fragment of quern, tiles, a bronze finger ring, bronze scales, coins (Arcadius, AD 383–395, and Theodosius II, AD 408–450), a blade from a pair of shears, an iron stylus, a number of large sarsen boulders, at least two of which appeared to be squared-off for building purposes, and what was thought to be part of a pillar made of Bath Stone. This indicated that Roman activity represented more than a local farmstead: instead, a large communal or corporate building must have been present. During this work a further well was spotted 182m to the east, which would place it on the floodplain, although it was not excavated.

While Mr Arnold was ploughing the same field in 1908, yet another well was discovered when one of his horses trod on it. This was most likely to have been the well initially noted by the Cunningtons. Excavation took place that year by Brooke just as soon as Mr Arnold had gathered in his crop of clover. Pottery and glass fragments were recovered, as well as animal bones, oyster shell, 'various bronze relics', and stone building material including a large number of sarsens and the base of a column. This was a very similar assemblage to that encountered in the previous well (and in Wilkinson's pit), and once again antler picks and flint flakes were amongst the collection. Brooke also recovered 33 coins, the dates of which led him to believe that the well was filled in 'while Valentinian I (AD 364–375) wore the purple'.[6] He drew attention to the presence of building material, worked stones, nails and roofing tiles. This well was 8m deep, and perhaps having learnt from his previous experience of excavating a well of this depth, he noted that he did not encourage visitors 'because of the great risk run to the men when working in a small deep space by interested individuals, who, leaning forward with craned necks, are not mindful of the danger caused by a stone falling on a man's head'.[7] Further wells have also been identified in the area, although these remain unexcavated and therefore undated; nonetheless it is interesting that a number seem to be grouped within a small area around Silbury Hill and the Swallowhead spring.

Excavations during the 20th century

Evidence for Roman activity continued to grow: when a trench for a sewer pipe was cut along the lower slope of Waden Hill, just east of the Winterbourne stream in 1926, it was observed by Cunnington who noted the presence of significant quantities of Roman material. In 1964, while investigating geological deposits exposed in the bank of the winterbourne stream to the east of Silbury Hill, John Evans, a lecturer at Cardiff University, noticed human bone eroding out of the side. An excavation ensued and the grave of a young man was revealed. His skull and neck bones had been washed away by the stream, but 30 hobnails were found at his feet, suggesting he was buried with his boots on. Pottery found within the grave fill places this burial in the later Roman period.[8] Only a few years later Atkinson's excavations of the large external ditch around Silbury uncovered a considerable amount of Romano-British pottery as well as over 100 4th-century coins, bone pins, and a bronze bracelet. All this was interpreted by Atkinson as rubbish derived from a small settlement.[9]

When the pipeline formerly observed by Cunnington was renewed in 1993, an excavation was undertaken. This confirmed the earlier observations and indicated the presence of five substantial stone buildings of Romano-British

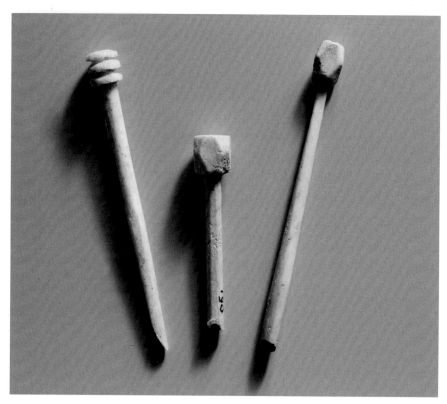

Roman pins excavated by Richard Atkinson from the Silbury Hill ditch. The longest one measures 50mm. (Courtesy Alexander Keiller Museum, Avebury. DP100097)

date, as well as a series of ditches and pits, although the very narrow trenches meant that only fragments were seen. Dating evidence from these excavations indicated that the majority of this assemblage, including the buildings, was of the later 3rd and 4th century, so from the final part of the Roman period, but a small amount of 1st- and 2nd-century pottery was also retrieved, suggesting that some form of settlement had existed there throughout the Romano-British period.[10] The opportunity to examine a larger area came a few years later during a routine check of aerial photographs by Mark Corney, then of the Royal Commission on the Historical Monuments of England. The photographs had been taken during the scorching summer of 1995; dry weather can often indicate the presence of buried archaeological features on arable land by affecting the growth of the crop growing above them, which when viewed from the air provides a plan of features buried beneath the ground. The parchmarks near the pipeline trench along Waden Hill indicated a far more extensive settlement than had previously been imagined, made up of at least 10 buildings set within a series of rectilinear enclosures laid either side of a road. In a publication in 1997, Corney was able to pull all the strands of Roman evidence together and suggested that there must be a Romano-British 'small town' around Silbury Hill.[11] By this time a number of Romano-British villages of varying sizes had been recognised on the higher downland of Salisbury Plain and the Marlborough Downs,[12] varying from simple farmsteads to massive settlements of several hundred houses. Most of these appeared to rely on local agriculture for subsistence, but one on Chapperton Down had developed along a significant routeway and may have relied upon passing trade. The Romano-British settlement at Silbury may have had a similar role.

The Silbury settlement revealed

Combined with the evidence from the 2006 and 2007 survey by the geophysics team, much of the settlement can now be described for the first time. Geophysics plots need to be interpreted; they require the eye of an experienced operator, and the data from around Silbury are no different, but there are some features that still stand out very clearly. To the south of Silbury Hill there is a grid pattern of roads: a central road leads north to south, perpendicular to the main road (the modern-day A4), with no less than two others at right angles, suggesting that at least part of it is a planned settlement. Numerous enclosure ditches are aligned with these roads and probably represent a mixture of field boundaries, property boundaries and paddocks. Clearly the enclosures are not all of a single phase as they overlie and overlap one another, representing varying sizes and shapes as needs and desires changed, and forming a palimpsest of activity, extending back perhaps to the beginning of the Roman period or even as early as the Iron Age. At least three stone-built buildings are evident from their prominent signatures on the survey. One sits in the middle of the settlement and is magnificently large: about the size of a 10-bedroom house today. The geophysical data suggest internal partitions within this house and hint at the presence of underfloor heating (a hypocaust). Just to the east of this is another stone building, somewhat smaller and simpler in size and design, and with no evidence for heating; it clearly had a different function or status. The third building, the smallest, lies just south of the road and was the structure originally seen on day one of the survey.

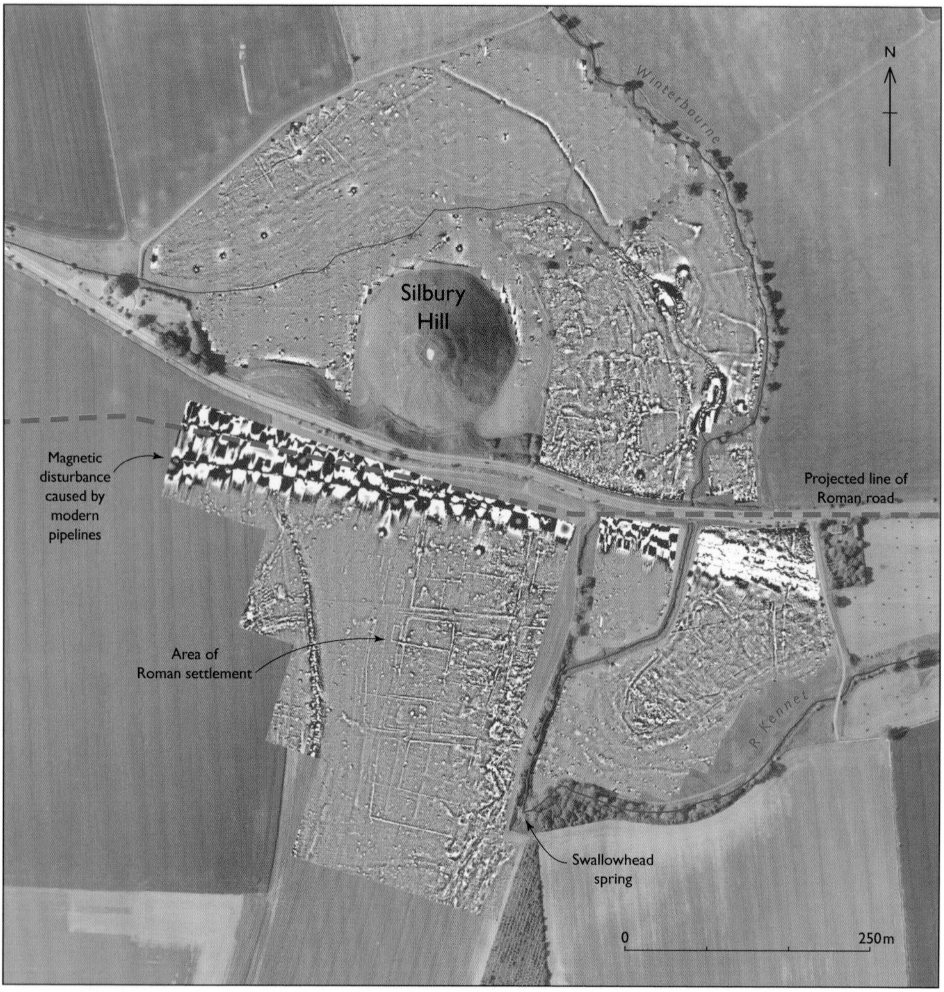
N
Winterbourne
Silbury Hill
Magnetic disturbance caused by modern pipelines
Projected line of Roman road
Area of Roman settlement
R. Kennet
Swallowhead spring
0
250m

The geophysical plot produced by the geophysics team. Silbury Hill is in the middle, and a grid pattern of roads is visible to the south.

Timber buildings no doubt also exist across this area, but are not picked up by magnetometry in the same way stone buildings are, and so might still lie silently undiscovered under the ploughsoil. Other features such as pits are dotted around the settlement, and anomalous readings in one area may suggest some sort of industrial activity, perhaps metalworking. Further to the geophysical work, the earthwork survey revealed a shallow, almost plough-levelled feature on the lower spur of Waden Hill south of the A4. This comprised an earthen bank no more than 500mm high forming an almost square enclosure. There was no direct evidence of date but given the proximity of the settlement, wells and other features, it was considered to date to the Romano-British period.

Interpreting the Silbury settlement

What all this activity means is difficult to say without further excavation. The artefacts recovered in the 19th and early 20th centuries from the wells and pits point to a late Roman date for most of the settlement, although a few fragments of 1st- and 2nd-century pottery were recorded. This is confirmed by the 1993 excavations along Waden Hill, which suggested that all the buildings were 3rd or 4th century.

The layout of this settlement suggests it was originally far more than a mere villa complex or village. The dense and complex networks of enclosures and a planned trackway system have the feel of an organic town about them, and the separate buildings, some on the grid of roads, suggest a degree of organisation and planning of the area to the south of the A4, with a more organic element alongside the Winterbourne stream. This settlement is undoubtedly akin to a Romano-British 'small town' as Corney has suggested. Situated alongside a main road, it was midway between the Roman settlements of Mildenhall and Sandy Lane and about a day's travel from both of them. It is also next to the river, which would have needed to be crossed, either by a bridge or ford, and therefore it is perhaps the natural place to break a journey and rest for the night. The settlement may therefore have started out as a *mutatio* (a relay station, as Corney suggests) or a *mansio* (a wayside inn); such places were often large structures with stables, a tavern and rooms to sleep, and it is not inconceivable that a settlement sprang up around it, benefiting from passing trade. The settlement was also located in an area of good agricultural land, and therefore farming may have played an important role. The inhabitants could have utilised the location next to the road to facilitate the distribution of agricultural products. It is equally possible, even likely, that it had an administrative role, perhaps the centre of a *pagus* (administrative district), as Andrew Reynolds of Institute of Archaeology, University College London, has suggested.[13]

The Roman town.

But there remains another intriguing element to this Romano-British settlement. Each day the inhabitants will have been confronted by the massive presence of Silbury Hill, and it is unthinkable that their lives were not affected by it. Indeed, it is the mound that appears to be the focus of attention rather than the Roman road, while its location next to the springs could provide added significance, suggesting that the settlement incorporated a religious component, as indeed many 'small towns' did. These normally took the form of wayside

shrines or religious buildings, offering travellers the opportunity to worship, but sometimes they included larger religious complexes such as those at Godmanchester (Cambs) or Springhead (Kent). The proximity of the Silbury settlement near to a number of springs is perhaps not a coincidence, as at some sites there are clear links between springs and ritual space. The temple complex at Springhead (as the name suggests) surrounded a whole series of natural springs, while the connection between the spring and the great temple at Bath is well known. Within the broader region of Silbury, it is probable that a major shrine is associated with a spring at Mother Anthony's Well,[14] and a Roman building exists close to springs at Cherhill, a little to the west. Votive offerings, such as coins, were also frequently cast into springs, perhaps to invoke or placate the power of the gods. At Bath, curses were written on small lead tablets and folded or rolled up before being cast into the sacred spring. Curses were generally a request from a victim of a crime to a deity to redress the balance by either exacting revenge on the wrongdoer (sometimes detailed in elaborate and gruesome detail) and/or by recovering the stolen item.

The Roman wells around Silbury are of interest and perhaps unusual given their close proximity to one another, and the numerous water sources. It may be that rather than being wells, they were ritual shafts – a feature often recorded in Roman Britain, where part of the 'backfill' actually represents votive offerings.[15] Based on their excavation, Brooke and Cunnington suggested that the well could have only been used for a relatively short period,[16] which is curious. It is interesting that both wells contained deer antlers and flint flakes. Is this a way of deliberately referencing their prehistoric predecessors? The concentration of coins recorded by Wilkinson in 1867 and again by Atkinson in 1968 suggests more of a votive deposit when viewed in this context. When we think again of the mass of pottery and metalwork that Wilkinson reported was discovered in the large pit excavated by A C Smith – could this carry with it a certain ritual element? After all, it did contain a fragment of human bone; hardly typical domestic debris. At the temple at Uley in Gloucestershire votive offerings, including curses, were deposited into a large, possibly water-filled pit within a temple. It could be that Wilkinson's pit was originally situated within a similar temple, the remains of which have been subsequently removed.

Continuing the religious theme, the settlement detected by the geophysical work to the north of the A4, around the base of Silbury Hill, has a very different layout to that along Waden Hill or in the fields to the south. It appears to show enclosures rather than rectilinear compounds as elsewhere, and one appears to have a circular structure inside it. Assuming that these features are contemporaneous with the rest of the settlement and not some earlier element, they could be interpreted as temple precincts surrounding the Hill. A possible temple was also recorded through geophysical survey on the top of Waden Hill in 1997.[17] Whatever the Romans were doing there it did clearly involve Silbury Hill, as indicated by the finds discovered on it, including a coin of Constantine the Great minted in Lyons between AD 335 and 345, found in a disturbed layer during the 2007 excavation on the summit, alongside a small quantity of Roman pottery. It should also be noted that, of the many round barrows to the east of Silbury on Overton Hill, at least three are of Roman date.[18] Perhaps the Romano-British inhabitants felt a greater connection with their ancestral landscape than with the distant Empire. The Silbury settlement was situated on the road to Bath, an important pilgrimage centre. Given the natural springs, coupled with the significance of the enormous mound, it may be that the Silbury settlement developed its own mythologies in the same way as Bath and became part of a pilgrimage route. Whatever its purpose, Silbury Hill dominated the lives of the people living in this settlement.

After the Romans

It is unknown what happened to this settlement after the Roman withdrawal from Britain in the 5th century. However, it is likely, given the artefactual evidence, that the focus of the town was diverted and, as in so many places, shifted. It may be that the settlement simply migrated and became Beckhampton. The paddocks and fields of the old, abandoned centre would have soon become overgrown and the buildings slowly reclaimed by nature; rotting timber rafters, no longer capable of supporting the roof, would have collapsed, exposing the building's interior to the weather, allowing weeds to grow through floor surfaces and out of the crumbling stonework.

People no doubt visited this decaying town: it certainly would have provided a ready supply of building stone and other materials for re-use in other houses. The derelict buildings could have provided a convenient, if slightly hazardous, shelter against the elements for shepherds or travellers, as well as for cattle and sheep. But, as an Anglo-Saxon hanging bowl mount found on the stream bed at the foot of Waden Hill suggests,[19] the Silbury settlement may also have been home to slightly longer-term, albeit small-scale, habitation.

Excavations around the West Kennet palisaded enclosures to the south-east of Silbury have recorded evidence of fairly extensive middle to late Anglo-Saxon activity [20] while a Late Anglo-Saxon stirrup mount was recovered from the bed of the River Kennet just south of Silbury.[21] Slightly further afield from Silbury but still only a short walk, a small early Anglo-Saxon settlement (6th century) existed to the south-west of Avebury henge monument. Excavations for the Avebury visitor car park recorded buildings typical of this period, known as 'Grubenhäuser' (or grub-huts to field archaeologists, who are prone to abbreviate and colloquialise) or the somewhat less loaded term 'Sunken Featured Buildings' (SFBs). These buildings, however, probably represent a loose collection of farmsteads rather than something we would recognise as a village or town. It is not until the Middle and Late Anglo-Saxon period (9th and 10th centuries) that the Avebury settlement seems to have grown considerably in size, developing into a town, and perhaps even a burh or fortified settlement.[22] Just as things can get bigger, so they can get smaller, and this may have been the case with Avebury where Andrew Reynolds has suggested that it was a failed small town, perhaps as a result of continued Viking raids.[23] But this forms part of a different story; one that is already set out in the splendid book *Avebury: The Biography of a Landscape*.[24]

Silbury Hill in the medieval period – a fortified site?

Despite lying in a politically strategic position, on the borderland between the kingdoms of Wessex and Mercia, Silbury itself seems to have been left alone for the few centuries after Roman rule, and it was not until the beginning of the 11th century that it once again became the focus of attention. For in the 11th century it appears to have been modified, its huge size perhaps providing a convenient look-out point along the old but still serviceable Roman road. The steps or terraces that can still be seen today near the summit may date to this time. Atkinson excavated a trench across the two uppermost terraces, revealing postholes along its inner vertical edge and associated with these were late Saxon or Norman pottery sherds, as well as a quarter cut from a silver penny minted around 1010, during the reign of Ethelred 'The Unready'. To Atkinson this was clearly an attempt to 'fortify Silbury as a strong-point against the Danes who were raiding deeply into southern England at this time from across the North Sea'.[25] Indeed, the Vikings did raid deep into this area as the *Anglo-Saxon Chronicles* record. In 878 the Vikings wintered at Chippenham and attacked settlements in Wessex. Battles were recorded at nearby Kennett in 1006 and another at Cannings Marsh in 1010.[26]

This idea of Silbury as an 11th-century fortification has been built upon more recently by Andrew Reynolds, who has suggested that the wider Avebury area was defended by a network of intervisible, and fortified signal stations connected by a military road, the 'herepath', with Silbury perhaps forming one of the signal stations. To Reynolds, the postholes Atkinson found on the terrace 'indicate a fortified site', while the name Silbury in Old English is Sele-burh, which can be interpreted as 'fortified structure or hall'.[27] However, the English Place-Name Survey places the emphasis on 'hall' and interprets the name as 'hall-barrow'. Whether the terracing was indeed an attempt to fortify the Hill is a moot point, since the topographical survey undertaken in 2001 clearly shows that the

A clipped silver coin of Ethelred (c. 968–
1016; little more than the size of a finger-
nail. (Courtesy Alexander Keiller Museum,
Avebury. DP100092)

terraces formed part of a spiral path up the hill rather than separate circuits.
They are therefore unlikely to be used for defensive palisades around the hill,
but are simply a way of getting to the top. Further, the postholes recorded by
Atkinson were only very slight, hardly capable of holding large palisade timbers.
They are better seen as revetting to keep the path clear of chalk.

Of course that does not mean that the hill remained undefended. After all, such
a substantial path around the hill implies that there was some serious activity
taking place on the summit at this period. Indeed, as mentioned earlier, it could
be that the top of the hill may have been truncated and flattened at this time, and
Roman paraphernalia swept away, in order to construct a building or palisade.
The spoil could easily have been thrown over the edge and subsequently eroded
down to be invisible to the eye today. This may explain the truncated appearance
of the prehistoric deposits on the summit and the lack of any stratigraphy later
than the prehistoric period (only a thin disturbed layer overlay the final stages of
construction of the mound). Although the burial Stukeley observed as being dug
up on the summit in 1723 is generally described as Viking, it is actually undated.
If the summit was modified in the early 11th century, the burial would need to
date to this time or later. During this work Stukeley acquired a horse-bit that may
have come from the top of the hill, and the drawing he made of it suggests that it
is possibly 11th century in date, as discussed in Chapter 2.

A few postholes were recorded cutting through the prehistoric deposits on the summit in the 2007 trench, most of which were small and ephemeral. However, one near the edge of the summit was really quite large (1m in diameter and at least 1m deep) and must have contained a post similar in size to a telegraph pole.

The large early medieval posthole recorded on the summit in 2007. This photograph does not really give you a sense of its true size, but it is truncated by Atkinson's trench on one side while much of the rest lies beyond the limit of excavation. The vertical scale is 1m long. (661-6178-91)

This is much more the size one would expect of a defensive palisade or perhaps a large building. The posthole had been sliced in half by Atkinson's trench to the east.[28] At the base of the posthole were broken fragments of sarsen stone, which would have been used as packing around the base of the post – presumably pieces conveniently re-used from the Neolithic deposits. Confusingly, two small sherds of Iron Age pottery were also recovered from this fill, but radiocarbon samples show us that it does date to between 900 and 1000 AD, and therefore may well relate to defensive action during the Viking raids.

Little else from the 2007 excavations can be precisely dated to the late 10th or early 11th centuries. A pit contained late 11th- to early 12th-century pottery. A medieval prick spur, which may well be mid-11th century, as well as two iron socketed arrowheads were recovered from the overlying topsoil. One of the arrowheads had a leaf-shaped blade and probably dates to the mid-13th century; the other was slender and could have been made anytime between the 11th and 14th centuries. Neither of these necessarily implies military activity. These finds suggest a general medieval presence, but probably after the Viking raids and not coeval with the large posthole or the supposed construction of the spiral path.

The stone bowl of Saxon or medieval date found on a ledge close to the base on the north side of the mound. Length 100mm. (Courtesy Alexander Keiller Museum, Avebury. DP100099)

They do, however, testify to the continued use of Silbury Hill. Other finds from Silbury are less well dated. A stone bowl, which may well be Saxon or medieval in date, was recovered by Atkinson from a cutting on one of the lower ledges on the north side of the hill. He also found a metal spearhead just next to the tunnel entrance in 1968.[29] This is now missing and therefore remains undated.

It is clear that Silbury Hill has had an extremely long history which has gradually moulded its shape over the generations into the form that comes down to us today – it is not a single-period monument, but the product of the whole of its past. Now in the modern era, Silbury is being recast again to be interpreted and re-interpreted by archaeologists and new agers; to be eulogised and rendered into stanzas; lauded and illustrated; captured by a thousand cameras. Silbury, however, remains a challenge.

Silbury Hill with a wooden palisade encircling the top in about the 10th century.

9 The timekeeper

Time, as measured by clocks, slips by so quickly. While no more than a few hours, days or weeks may have passed by since you started reading this book, it is surprising to all those involved with Silbury Hill since the hole appeared in its surface that so many years have passed by. The Hill has during that time undergone a comprehensive archaeological review. Another phase of activity in the long life of the monument has engraved its tale on the mound and its interior. The degree to which this will be detectable on the surface by future archaeologists searching for clues to the activities of earlier investigations remains to be seen. Nevertheless, it has made a contribution to the process of change that can be seen to have taken place over the past 4,500 years.

During that time there have been a number of transformations, with several manifestations that we can only guess at. Those who started the pile of gravel at the junction of chalk and valley floor will not have known what was to follow. They could not have realised that periods of construction and modification would result in a complete metamorphosis of the site. Similarly, over time, activities and events ebbed and flowed around the landscape with, at one point, a whole town being constructed at the foot of the mound. Whether the Romans who lived there ever dug into the heart of the mound is, for now, unknown, but they may well have been responsible for a number of activities on its summit and slopes. Given the kind of burial monuments that traditionally occur outside towns across the Roman Empire, it would be surprising if it was not covered in shrines and other paraphernalia. It is unlikely that the Neolithic builders or Roman pilgrims would be concerned that, millennia later, so many people visit the mound or that they treat it in a symbolic or religious way. They will not, however, have ever imagined that people would be so interested in digging to the centre simply to find a rich burial. Times change, as they say.

Changing perceptions and different imaginings

As times have changed so perceptions of the Hill have changed. It has, no doubt, always demanded some form of explanation. Aubrey, in the mid-17th century, relates the local tradition that the mound was raised over the burial of King Sil sitting on horseback.[1] By the late 19th century the burial had become that of a man in golden armour on horseback,[2] or a King buried in a golden coffin.[3] Given the enormous size of Silbury, it is understandable that the presumed burial was thought to be that of a king.

Folklore associated with Silbury Hill tends to be a little more colourful. One tradition has it that while the devil was making the Wansdyke, he cleaned his spade and the loose earth formed the mound.[4] A variation of this was told by 'a native of Melksham' to the folklorist Robert Heanley:

> When Stonehenge was builded, a goodish bit after Avebury, the devil was in a rare taking. 'There's getting a vast deal too much religion in these here parts,' he says, 'summat must be done.' So he picks up his shovel, and cuts a slice out of Salisbury Plain, and sets off for to smother up Avebury. But the priests saw him coming and set to work with their charms and incusstations, and they fixed him while he was yet a nice way off, till at last he flings down his shovelful just where he was stood. And THAT'S Silbury.[5]

Yet another tradition has it that it all started as a fight between the townspeople of Devizes and Marlborough (or Avebury – the towns vary according to allegiances). Marlborough, seeking revenge for having been thoroughly beaten by Devizes, requested the help of the Devil. The Devil obliged and took up a great hill to dump over Devizes. St John, however, on hearing of the Devil's plans, rushed to Devizes. He told everyone to bring out their old shoes and clothes, which he put in a huge sack and gave to the oldest man. The old man set out towards the Devil and they met at Beckhampton, 'How far is it to Devizes?' asked the Devil. 'Could I reach it by night?' 'Oh no,' replied the old man, 'it is very, very far away. I set out as a young man and these,' he said emptying the sack, 'are all the shoes and clothes I've worn out on the way.' The Devil, not wishing to walk such a distance, flung down the hill where he was; Devizes was saved and Silbury created.[6] There are numerous variations on this story, the towns and people involved changing with each story, the result of generations of re-telling, and in fact other hills have similar legends attached to them (notably the Wrekin in Shropshire).

A legend of Silbury Hill, depicting the old man fooling the Devil by showing him his sack of old shoes. Linocut by Denis Grant-King. (Courtesy of WANHS)

Such folklore is often parabolic and can easily enter the public psyche. David Collison, the Producer of the Silbury *Chronicle* documentary, recalls mentioning to some farmhands in the Red Lion that they were about to start digging into Silbury, only to be told ,'You'll find naught in there but some old boots and shoes.'[7] Indeed, Atkinson's excavations led to a certain revival of such legends, and it is no coincidence that only a year after his investigations *Dr Who and the Daemons* was broadcast, in which an archaeologist excavates into 'Devil's Hump' burial mound and unwittingly (and despite the Doctor's protestations) unleashes Azal, the last of the Daemons. Filming is still popularly recalled as having taken place in a village local to the Marlborough Downs.

Although conventional archaeological interpretations have rarely engaged with folklore, such 'traditional' meanings of sites have often been drawn on to provide alternative understandings. And indeed unconventional approaches themselves can become a sort of modern folklore, seeping into the literature and drifting in and out of the general consciousness, until the monument becomes inextricably entwined with these ideas, whether a Mother Goddess, harvest hill or the centre point of a web of ley-lines. And as with most things in life, these alternative interpretations change according to the fashion and over time.

In contrast to the cautious explanations of archaeologists, and with a potent blend of folklore, archaeology, ancient history and a substantial dose of speculation, Michael Dames's theory has had a great deal more impact than conventional interpretations. The central thesis of Dames's 1976 book *The Silbury Treasure: The Great Goddess Rediscovered* is that Silbury Hill (and the surrounding ditch and ditch extension) is a massive representation of a pregnant Mother Goddess. Based on the evidence of Atkinson's supposed flying ants and the associated (but unprovable) suggestion that the Hill was constructed in August, he argues that a harvest festival was celebrated at Silbury.[8] J D Wakefield developed this idea further, suggesting that the (post-medieval) ditches and water meadows immediately north of Silbury also represent an image of the 'Silbury Hag'.[9] Latterly, Paul Devereux has argued that Silbury was very precisely located since the summit can be seen from other monuments in the surrounding area, with the upper terrace appearing at the same level as the horizon.[10] Others have claimed that the Hill represents a giant sundial; its shadow indicating the time or the season. More recently a 'sun roll' effect has been claimed, whereby twice a year, when viewed from a particular location inside the broadly contemporary West Kennet palisaded enclosure complex, the setting sun appears to roll down the side of the mound.[11] Frequently, the mound figures in ley-line based theories; the latest, that of Tom Brooks, has argued that prehistoric monuments form a series of isosceles triangles spiralling out from Silbury Hill. Rather than seeing blurred and distorted fragments of the past, he sees prehistoric sites as a series of neat dots on a map and therefore a pattern is sought.[12]

A more controversial idea, in *Silbury Dawning: The Alien Visitor Gene Theory* by John Cowie, is that Silbury Hill was constructed 13,000 years ago by intelligent alien visitors who passed on some of their genes, and therefore intelligence, to the resident Homo sapiens population (the original summer of love).[13] While these varied interpretations raise a multitude of archaeological problems, not least the propensity to favour the final form of the monument at the expense of its complex development and evolution, some theorists have struck a chord where archaeological interpretations have failed to ignite the imagination. They have become an alternative but prominent part of the modern folklore of the Hill.

The sanctity of the monument is clear in many of these modern interpretations. One only need wander down to the Swallowhead spring, just south of Silbury, to see how Dames's influential book has become tradition. The rags hanging from the willow tree, to say nothing of the other votive offerings around the springhead – crystals, candles, wind chimes to mention but a few – announce that you are entering contemporary sacred ground. The willow has now cracked forming an arch, creating a sort of portal one has to go through, which helps to give the impression that you are entering a different realm. It has been suggested that this modern ritual activity is a direct result of the publication of Dames's *The Silbury Treasure*, which connected the spring with the Great Goddess.[14] Gatherings of women on the top of Silbury Hill since the 1980s have also been inspired by Dames. Dancing during the August full moon, the women celebrate the harvest festival, fertility, femininity and that feminine icon – the

The Swallowhead spring, looking south. The spring is directly ahead, with the water trickling under the arching willow tree and forming the River Kennet just behind the camera. (661-6306-09)

Great Goddess.[15] As Jon Cannon put it: 'Michael Dames and others are creating myths that have the persuasive power to make people feel spiritually connected to the Downs and their former inhabitants, engaging people with the Avebury landscape at a deep level.'[16]

Rock musician and writer Julian Cope has made these and other ideas relevant to a new generation. With considerable archaeological insight he has successfully fused antiquity with rock music. Silbury becomes one of a number of sacred hills, and the 'Mother Hill' takes pride of place on the mythological mind map.[17] Noting Richard Gough's description of 'a rotten post',[18] he kept one step ahead and identified the site as that of Yggdrasil, the tree of life of the Vikings. Yggdrasil was central to Norse cosmology and appears to have derived from shamanic belief. Its branches reached to heaven and spread over the earth and its three roots were fed by two springs and a well or lake. Water and mud from one of the springs was tipped daily over the tree by attendants to keep the branches from rotting. The tree was surrounded by nine worlds although what form these took is unclear.[19]

These modern interpretations are creating a new set of beliefs. Pagan and new age communities see Silbury and the surrounding landscape as sacred; to be treated with due regard and reverence. In this respect this may be a pastiche of a process first started in the Neolithic, and one that would not have been unfamiliar in the Roman period. To Edward Drax the monument was a relict of 'the old Patriarchal Religion', and it is no coincidence that of the antiquarians during the 1849 investigation, two were clergymen. So the Hill has frequently had religious or sacred connotations. Druids, Wiccans and other pagans have become a familiar sight at prehistoric, particularly Neolithic, monuments. They actively engage with them, and votive offerings (drawing directly from folkloric traditions) are evident at most. At Silbury, Terry Dobney (better known as Terry the Druid) who is the self-appointed Archdruid of Avebury and Keeper of the Stones, conducts a harvest festival on Silbury Hill on the first day of every August (an example of how the ideas of Dames have percolated into other modern pagan traditions).

Votive offerings around the mouth of Swallowhead spring – small replica pots, a stick person and the remains of wax candles. These offerings change day by day. (661-6306-13)

However, while there is an emphasis in the literature on the colourful but unconventional activities of a few, the perceptions and beliefs of the majority remain silent. In December each year, St James's church in Avebury hosts a service of light. There is no electric light, just candles held by the congregation which cast flickering shadows around the walls of the Saxon nave. While most concentrate on their devotions, the process focuses attention on the cave-like structure of the church, with its small circular windows set high in the wall. Although larger in scale, the church is not that dissimilar to the passage in the chambered long barrow of West Kennet. Both face east towards the rising sun. It is intriguing to think that the Avebury monuments may have witnessed such cultural and spiritual changes in the past, and indeed the very origins of Silbury Hill may be rooted in such change. That the monuments, both prehistoric and historic, are witness to changing belief systems ensures that there is something here for everyone. In one way or another all may identify with the place. Today the inhabitants and visitors to Avebury are multi-cultural in background and multi-religious in belief, and the extent to which interpretations and conservation strategies will differ and how these various interests will impact on the site in years to come we can only guess at.

Other modern ways of understanding and interpreting the Hill have come through various art forms; poetry, painting, sculpture, music and literature. These are a way of expressing a relationship with the monument, of describing an individual's inner vision of it and an attempt to capture the spirit of the place. This is certainly a viable alternative to the often apparently dull archaeological interpretations, but read together, these two approaches, archaeological and artistic, can harmonise and complement one another. As examples by Robert Southey and Emmeline Fisher show, Silbury has attracted its fair share of poetic expression from the early 19th century to the modern day.

The artist Paul Nash painted Silbury Hill twice in the mid 1930s. The Hill provided him 'with an image of geometric mass in the landscape, amplified by a mystical rather than historical resonance'.[20] In 1937 artist John Piper (who had been a member of the Wiltshire Archaeological and Natural History Society as a boy) compared an aerial photograph of Silbury to the paintings of Miró.[21]

Emphasising movement, artist Richard Long created a temporary art work in the Whitechapel Art Gallery in 1971, formed of a solid circular spiral of muddy boot prints and entitled 'A line the same length as a straight walk from the bottom to the top of Silbury Hill'. For artist David Inshaw, a founder member of the 'Brotherhood of Ruralists', Silbury Hill 'seems to me to convey in a very dramatic way, and in a way no natural structure could, all the problems of reconciling the moment with a larger grasp of time. Its extraordinary presence acts as a timeless focus for man's efforts to understand his environment'.[22] Inshaw's work 'Silbury Hill in the Moonlight' is used as the cover of this book; and the text of this book and the painting can be seen as complementary. Contemporary composer Sir Harrison Birtwistle drew directly from archaeological inspiration when he composed 'Silbury Air' – a non-romantic composition for chamber ensemble. Written in 1977, it is his 'reaction to that place'.[23]

In his partially autobiographical 1922 book *The Secret Places of the Heart*, H G Wells used Silbury Hill (as well as Avebury and Stonehenge) as the place to come to unwind from the stresses of London; to take stock, to slow down, to sit on the summit of the Hill and say things 'very learned and inconclusive about the exact purpose of this vast heap of chalk and earth, this heap that men had made before the temples at Karnak were built or Babylon had a name'. He contrasts this with the activities of archaeologists: ' "Clumsy treasure hunting," Sir Richmond said. "They bore into Silbury Hill and expect to find a mummified chief or something sensational of that sort, and they don't, and they report nothing ... These archaeologists don't know. Or if they do they haven't told me, which is just as bad. I don't believe they know." '[24]

In time with Silbury

In her book of Avebury village memories published in 1999, Marjorie Rawlins resignedly lamented the changes of the 1920s. She recalled how local people initially benefited from the business that the archaeologists brought with them. But there were soon repercussions as Alexander Keiller, who purchased the manor, cleared away cottages built of sarsen and tidied up the stone circle. He even used explosives to clear away bushes and trees and level off the bank in the north-west quadrant so that it was more presentable. The village was never the same as the trickle of visitors slowly increased. Elements of traditional village life lingered on until finally the school closed in 2007. Along with St James's church, this had formed the heart of the community and provided local people with a reference point that they would carry with them throughout their later life and in turn pass on to their children. It was the social glue that helped to define the village as a place of substance. Now Avebury, and Silbury Hill with it, has entered a new millennium and the monuments perform a new role. The landscape responds to European Union grants, the villages resonate with planning applications, commuters, new age disciples and crop circle investigators. The beer in the Red Lion pub no longer comes from the local brewery. In these respects the area is no different from countless other villages, except that numerically, the villagers of Avebury are far outnumbered by visitors, and the major features of village infrastructure are car parks, access routes and other facilities. Here the important component of the scenery is people negotiating footpaths, meadows and often, it has to be said, cultivated fields.

The great difference now is that Avebury and its monuments are legally protected, recognised by UNESCO as of significant international scientific and cultural value, and this places great responsibility on conservationists to manage the area carefully. Inevitably, this is sometimes difficult to achieve given the conflicting pressures of modern life. Could Avebury have a telephone mast erected in its midst? No, it would detract from the landscape setting of the site. Consequently, Avebury inhabitants now find themselves in a modern communications black hole, at least as far as mobile phones are concerned. On the face of it the whole point of the area is now to generate tourism. In some cases this is fuelled by the public's continuing interest in archaeology and a general curiosity in the mythologies or 'mysteries' of the past, while to others it is simply a place for a good day out, somewhere to go to relieve the stress of modern life – like a trip to the cinema.

But there is another side to this, for many are curiously attracted to the place. While it is equally possible to visit somewhere with modern comforts, roofed over and with warmth, many feel compelled to travel to the area, often in the depth of winter, and, procession-like, circumnavigate and touch the stones at Avebury and then make their way to Silbury Hill and the West Kennet long barrow. This is as much a pilgrimage as for those who visit Lourdes. The monuments serve a social and spiritual need. They provide a valuable link and connection with the distant past and with its roots.

Indeed, there is an inherent desire to meet and speak to our ancestors. However our yearning to speak with people from another time does not just extend backwards into the past, but also forwards into the future. In an attempt to speak to a later generation, Richard Falkner placed a stoneware jar at the centre of the mound and another at the entrance at the conclusion of the 1849 tunnelling into Silbury Hill. As has already been described, the central one (with the poem by Emmeline Fisher) was recovered by Professor Atkinson in 1969. In turn, Atkinson left a calling card in the portal, and his colleagues at the BBC left a box of goodies for future explorers; they could hardly have foreseen that their box would have been retrieved in their own lifetime. Contact made; they had spoken to a later generation. For us the artefacts from earlier time capsules are tangible contact with people from the past; they provide details of their lives and of the things that they did.

And so in our own time too was the idea of a time capsule to be placed in the Hill mooted. Local children were asked by English Heritage to put things that they felt represented aspects of their lives inside a Kilner jar, with the aim of burying it in the tunnel backfill. The schoolchildren loved the idea. But there was protest from many other places – it contradicted the ethos of the project given that the conceit of a time capsule is that one day it should be dug up, while some saw this as an intrusion into a sacred site and evidence of the intention to disturb the site yet again in the future. In the end the time capsule was placed in the Alexander Keiller Museum alongside the contents of the earlier time capsules. Preserved in the archive, the children's objects, pictures and letters will speak to future generations in the years to come in a different way.

Silbury, however, is its own time capsule; open and forever being added to – a repository of memories and actions past and present, and a stage for those still to come. While the names of those who built the mound or of the miners who later dug the shaft into it are now lost, the genealogy is provided by their actions in the monument itself; its various phases and episodes are tangibly encapsulated in those fragments of artefacts that were left behind. The mound incorporates the activities, the behaviour and performance of people, the building of banks, ditches and mounds; basketful after basketful of actions that provide a biography of the local inhabitants. It is as good as any family tree. We are all a part of that dialogue, and our actions form part of the same story.

Blue moon

It was New Year's Eve, a few months after our work had drawn to a close at Silbury Hill. Avebury was relatively subdued. It was a beautiful night, brightly lit by a blue moon; the second full moon of the month. A thin bank of cirrus obscured all but the brightest of stars, and occasionally gave the moon an incandescent halo. The luminous glow cast strong shadows and gave new form to the undulations on the sarsens. It seemed to bring the stones to life. New shapes came into perspective, their form only restricted by the individual imagination of the observer. This must be how they were meant to be seen. At the same time the henge bank ensured that focus lay upon the immediate area, and only the streetlight opposite the Red Lion distracted attention. It was cold, zero degrees, but it felt colder. A small group of people from Bradford-on-Avon conducted a ritual at each stone in turn; placing lanterns in front of the sarsens, a cut-out paper swan positioned in a niche; and then collectively making a wish while tapping the stone with impromptu magic wands – an improvised 21st-century ritual. Big Ben, that modern timepiece, was not audible here, but the peal of bells that had been ringing from

A full moon over Silbury Hill. (Photo: © Pete Glastonbury)

St James's church halted momentarily in order to sound off the seconds. Shouts and cheers from inside the British Legion and Parish Hall heralded the Midnight Hour, while the group from Bradford exchanged hugs and symbolic presents and recited an Ode to the New Year. Two individuals preferred to hug the trees with their enormous root systems that bind the east terminal of the henge bank, while simultaneously, several paper lanterns were lit, some of which rose spectacularly, taking their messages high into the night sky. Silbury Hill was dark and silent. It had provided the backdrop to these events before.

The timekeeper

Notes

Chapter 1

1   As in Jackson 1862, 333; Long 1858, 339–40
2   Dames 1976; 1977
3   Cope 1998, 202
4   Such as in Dames 1976
5   For Leland's itinerary, *see* Toulmin Smith 1964
6   Camden 1806, 136
7   Simmonds 2008, 68
8   Rawlins 1999, 30. Presumably this was the partial eclipse of 1927
9   Stukeley 1743, 43–4
10 Hoare 1821, 80
11 Parslew 2004, 42
12 Devizes Museum, WAHNS Library Cuttings 4: 155
13 Devizes Museum, WAHNS Library Cuttings 13: 263
14 Parslew 2004, 53
15 Rawlins 1999
16 Gingell 1996, 510

Chapter 2

1   Jackson 1862, 316; Fowles 1980, 22
2   Stukeley 1743, 43, based on fieldwork of the 1720s
3   Welfare 1989
4   Jackson 1862, 332; Fowles 1980, 682
5   Quoted from Ucko *et al* 1991, 265–6
6   Anon 1862; Jackson 1862, opp p 320; Fowles 1980, 48–9, 683
7   Fowles 1980, 680–1. A posnet is a type of cooking pot. The reference to Silbury being raised while a 'posnet of milk was seething' is difficult to interpret. Aubrey could have been suggesting that he thought it was built during a feast, or that it was perhaps built very rapidly, that is, in the time it takes to boil milk. Alternatively, it may have been a biblical reference: 'Thou shalt not see the a kid in his mother's milk' (Exodus 23:19), and similar examples can be found elsewhere in the Bible, perhaps reflecting a belief that the Hill was built at the time of Moses
8   Fowles 1980, 682
9   Stukeley 1743, 44
10 Lukis 1887, 246
11 Stukeley 1743, 41, 42
12 Pollard and Reynolds 2002, 227. Quita Mould (pers comm) has recently also identified it from the illustration as 11th century
13 Douglas 1793, 161
14 Tucker 1851, 298
15 Mortimer 2003, 4
16 Hutton 2009, 89–90
17 Ucko *et al* 1991, 89
18 Crittall 1975, 73; Pugh 1965, 161
19 Society of Antiquaries of London minutes, dated 27 Thursday June 1776
20 Douglas 1793, 161
21 Camden 1789, 110
22 British Library MS Add 34813 ff110–12: *see* Edwards 2010 for a transcription of the letters
23 Demidoff 1773
24 *Salisbury and Winchester Journal* Monday 23 December 1776
25 Cannon and Constantine 2004, 78–9
26 Buchanan and Cossins 1969, 88; Jones and Chown 1977, 22; Latimer 1893, 78–9, 275
27 Bodleian MS Library Gough Maps 231 fol 216
28 Merewether 1851a, 74
29 Devizes Museum DD14; Edwards 2002
30 Pass 1887, 252
31 Merewether 1851a, 74
32 Tucker 1851, opp p 297
33 Merewether 1851a, 75
34 Tucker 1851, 301
35 Tucker 1851, 300
36 Merewether 1851a, 80

37 Merewether 1851a, 75–6

38 Merewether 1851b, 97

39 When Emmeline Fisher was young.
she spent time with Wordsworth and he
took an interest in her writing. Through
this connection, she was invited to craft
an alternate national anthem on the
occasion of Queen Victoria's coronation.
While Fisher's anthem was not used, it
did earn her the attention of the young
queen, who sent Fisher a boxed writing
set. Fisher published one volume of
poems in 1856 under her married name,
Emmeline Hinxman, and she published
a series of poems in *Fraser's Magazine* in
the early 1860s. With her Silbury poem,
Fisher joins a small body of Victorian
poets who focus on archaeology, among
them Thomas Hardy who also wrote
about the prehistoric monuments of
Salisbury Plain. The poem left in the
Silbury Hill tunnel differs slightly
from a version published in the
*Wiltshire Archaeological and Natural
History Magazine* **1** (1854). The above
information has been supplied by
Virginia Zimmerman, who also supplied
the following transcription (which
differs from that published recently in
British Archaeology **98**):
Bones of our wild forefathers, O forgive,
If now we pierce the chambers of your rest,
And open your dark pillows to the eye
Of the irreverent Day! Hark, as we move,
Runs no stern whisper through the narrow
    vault?
Flickers no shape across our torchlight pale
With backward beckoning arm? No, all is still.
O that it were not! O that sound or sign,
Vision, or legend, or the eagle glance
Of science, could call back thy history lost,
Green Pyramid of the plains, from far-ebbed
    Time!
O that winds which kiss thy flowery turf
Could utter how they first beheld thee rise;
When in his soil the zealous Savage paused,
Drew deep his chest, pushed back his yellow
    hair,

And scanned the growing hill with reverent
    gaze, –
Or haply, how they gave their fitful pipe
To join the chant-prolonged o'er warrior
    cold. –
Or how the Druid's mystic robe they swelled;
Or from thy blackened brow on wailing wing
The solemn sacrificial ashes bore,
To strew them where now smiles the yellow
    Corn.
Or where the peasant treads this Churchward
    path.

40 Tucker 1851, 301, 303

41 Article on Stonehenge and Avebury in
Quarterly Review July 1860

42 Wilkinson 1869, 114–15

43 Wilkinson 1869, 115

44 Wilkinson 1869, 115–16

45 Wilkinson 1869, 117

46 Pass 1887, 248

47 Pass 1887, 250

48 Pass 1887, 252

49 Pass 1887, 251

50 Hutton 2009, 298

51 Anon 1881, 21

Chapter 3

1 Alexander Keiller Museum: Atkinson
archive

2 *Marlborough Times* 24 August 1962

3 A D Passmore MS in the Wiltshire
Archaeological and Natural History
Society Museum, Devizes

4 Petrie 1924, 215

5 Petrie 1924, 216

6 Passmore 1920, 185–6; Petrie 1924, 217

7 Atkinson 1978, 159

8 David Collison, pers comm

9 McKim 1959

10 Wiltshire Local Studies Library R SIL
930; Atkinson also prepared a general
account of the project design for the
BBC (1968) and another for the
archaeological community (1967)

11 Wiltshire Local Studies Library R SIL
930; Long 1858, 340; Smith 1862, 181

12 Wiltshire Local Studies Ref Library R SIL

930; Atkinson 1967

13 Atkinson 1956, 167

14 Alexander Keiller Museum: Atkinson archive

15 Wiltshire Local Studies Library R SIL 930; Atkinson 1967, 259

16 Wiltshire Record Office 3293/1 Letter from *Nature Conservancy* 10 September 1964

17 Atkinson 1978, 162

18 Atkinson 1978, 162

19 Atkinson 1978, 166

20 Robinson 1997, 41

21 Atkinson 1978, 172

22 Alexander Keiller Museum, Silbury Hill archive, letter from Atkinson to A J Taylor 15 January 1969

23 Clough and Cummins 1988, 160, 162

24 Wiltshire Record Office Lord Avebury papers 3293/1

25 Atkinson 1978

26 Several interim accounts (1967, 1968 and 1969b) were produced by Atkinson as the excavations progressed, and the full account was published by Alasdair Whittle in 1997

Chapter 4

1 *Bristol Journal* 2 November 1776

2 *Wiltshire Gazette & Herald* 19 April 2001

3 *Western Daily Press* 3 April 2001, 19

4 *The Times Higher Education Supplement* 11 May 2001, 55

5 *The Times Magazine* 9 June 2001, 20–6

Chapter 5

1 Atkinson 1969a

2 Atkinson 1969a

3 Tucker 1851, 300; Merewether 1851a, 79

4 *Chronicle* documentary July 1969

5 Whittle 1997, 13

6 Atkinson 1978, 166, 172

7 Atkinson 1969a, 77

8 Keiller 1939, 232; Wainwright 1971, 190

9 Whittle 1997, 22

10 Anon 1862; Fowles 1980, 48–9, 683; Jackson 1862, opp p 320

Chapter 6

1 Renfrew 1973

2 Barrett 1994, 29–31

3 As pointed out by Whittle 1997, 147

4 Edward Drax in a letter to George Pitt, 4 November 1776; Edwards 2010

5 Quennell and Quennell 1907, 72

6 Atkinson 1978

7 Parker Pearson 1993, 71

8 Whittle 1997, 148, 150, 151

9 Woodward and McDonald 2002, 53–66

10 Hall 1997, 18–23

11 Hall 1997, 18–23; Charles *et al* 2004, 59–60

12 Irwin 1982, 347

13 Hall 1997, 18 uses the term 'authors of the mound'

14 Scarre 2004

15 Owoc 2001; 2004

16 Pass 1887, 248–9

17 Taylor 1951, 162

18 Darling 1998

19 Bell *et al* 1996, 13–16

20 There is a wide range of literature dealing with North American mounds, among them Milner 2004, and Woodward and McDonald 2002. Topping 2010 provides a useful introduction, while Iseminger 2010 is a good introduction to Monk's Mound, the largest in North America.

21 Barnett 1998

22 Słupecki 2006, 127–8

23 Hall 1995

24 Anon 1993

Chapter 7

1 Smith 1884

2 For example, Allen 2005, 100–1

3 Field 2005, 88–9

4 Ashbee *et al* 1979, 283

5   Bayliss *et al* 2007

6   Whittle *et al* 1999

7   Gillings *et al* 2008, 9–24

8   Pollard and Cleal 2004, 121

9   Whittle 1997, 53–86

10 Gillings *et al* 2008, 73

11 Barber 2003, 128

12 Fitzpatrick 2009, 183–4; *also* Field
    2008, 92 – zone of information

13 Parker Pearson *et al* 2009, 31–3

14 Hoare 1821, 5–6

15 Tilley 1994

16 *See* Richards 1996a and 1996b for a
    good discussion of late Neolithic
    monuments and water

Chapter 8

1   Lukis 1887, 245

2   Wilkinson 1869, 114–16, 117

3   Pass 1887, 252

4   Brooke and Cunnington 1896

5   Brooke and Cunnington 1896

6   Brooke 1910, 374

7   Brooke 1910, 375

8   Evans 1966

9   Atkinson 1978, 172

10 Powell *et al* 1996

11 Corney 1997

12 Fowler 2000, 95–7; Fowler and
    Blackwell 1998, 67–72; McOmish *et al*
    1999

13 Reynolds 2005

14 Corney and Walters 2001

15 A point already stated by Corney and
    Walters 2001, 24–5

16 Brooke and Cunnington 1896, 170

17 Pollard and Reynolds 2002, 233

18 Cleal 2005; Pollard and Reynolds 2002,
    176–7

19 Youngs 1998

20 Pollard and Reynolds 2002; Whittle
    1997, 93

21 Robinson 1992

22 Pollard and Reynolds 2002; Reynolds
    2001

23 Pollard and Reynolds 2002; Reynolds
    2001

24 Pollard and Reynolds 2002

25 Atkinson 1978, 170

26 Swanton 2000, 137, 141

27 Pollard and Reynolds 2002, 227

28 Indeed this posthole should have been
    clearly visible to Atkinson's team in their
    western section, but Atkinson noted that
    this trench 'revealed no trace of post-
    Neolithic structures' (Atkinson 1970,
    314)

29 *Chronicle* documentary July 1969

Chapter 9

1   Fowles 1980, 680–1; Brian Edwards
    (pers comm) suggests that the name
    'King Sil' could also be a corruption of
    King's Hill

2   Smith 1862; Law and Crooke 1900, 347

3   Burne 1915

4   Gomme 1909, 80

5   Heanley 1913

6   Smith 1862

7   David Collison, pers comm

8   Dames 1976, 41, 85

9   Wakefield 1999, 55–60

10 Devereux 1991

11 Marshall, S and Currie, G forthcoming
    'The Silbury sun-roll'. *Time and Mind*

12 Brooks 2002; 2006

13 Cowie 2002

14 Cannon 2005

15 Cannon 2005; Bender 1998, 185

16 Cannon 2005, 206

17 Cope 1998; *also* map insert with Cope's
    1996 album *Interpreter*, Echo Records

18 Camden 1789, 110: Cope's 'The
    Road to Yggdrasilbury' (track 5 on the
    CD *Discover Odin*, The British Museum:
    Head Heritage 12) makes the link
    between Silbury and Viking mythology

19 Brondsted 1975, 271–3

20 Hauser 2007, 128

21 Hauser 2007, 15

22 Simmonds 2008, 80

23 Pitts 2009

24 Wells 1922, 93–4

References

Allen, S 2005 'Mesolithic hunter gatherers exploitation of the Marlborough Downs' *in* Brown,G, Field, D and McOmish, D (eds) *The Avebury Landscape: Aspects of Field Archaeology in the Marlborough Downs*. Oxford: Oxbow, 95–102

Anon 1862 'Facsimiles of Aubrey's plans of Abury Wilts'. *Wiltshire Archaeol Natur Hist Mag* **7**, 224–7

Anon 1881 'The twenty-fifth annual meeting of the Wiltshire Archaeological and Natural History Society at Marlborough 1879'. *Wiltshire Archaeol and Natur Hist Soc* **19**, 1–23

Anon 1993 *Tinatare – Temple of Heaven*. Beijing: Esperanto Press

Ashbee, P, Smith, I F and Evans, J G 1979 'Excavation of three long barrows near Avebury, Wiltshire'. *Proc Prehistory Soc* **45**, 207–300

Atkinson, R J C 1956 (1990 edn) *Stonehenge*. London: Penguin

Atkinson, R J C 1967 'Silbury Hill'. *Antiquity* **41**, 259–62

Atkinson, R J C 1968 *Silbury Hill*. London: BBC

Atkinson, R J C 1969a 'A season at Silbury'. *The Listener*, 16 January 1969, 76–7

Atkinson, R J C 1969b 'The date of Silbury Hill'. *Antiquity* **43**, 216

Atkinson, R J C 1970 'Silbury Hill, 1969–70'. *Antiquity* **44**, 313–14

Atkinson, R J C 1978 'Silbury Hill' *in* Sutcliffe, R (ed) *Chronicle: Essays from Ten Years of Television Archaeology*. (London: BBC), 159–73

Barber, M 2003 *Bronze and the Bronze Age: Metalwork and Society in Britain c2500–800 BC*. Stroud: Tempus

Barnett, J 1998 *The Natchez Indians*. Natchez: Mississippi Dept of Archives and History

Barrett, J C 1994 *Fragments from Antiquity*. Oxford: Blackwell

Bayliss, A, Whittle, A and Wysocki, M 2007 'Talking about my generation: the date of the West Kennet long barrow' *in* Bayliss, A and Whittle, A (eds) *Histories of the Dead: Building Chronologies for Five Southern British Long Barrows* (Supplement to Cambridge Archaeol J **17**, 1). Cambridge: Cambridge University Press

Bell, M, Fowler, P J and Hillson, S W 1996 *The Experimental Earthwork Project: 1960–1992*. (Counc Brit Archael Res Rep **100**). York: Counc Brit Archaeol

Bender, B 1998 *Stonehenge: Making Space*. Oxford: Berg

Brondsted, J 1975 *The Vikings*. Harmondsworth: Penguin

Brooke, J W 1910 'The excavations of a Roman well near Silbury Hill, October 1908'. *Wiltshire Archaeol Natur Hist Mag* **36**, 373–5

Brooke, J W and Cunnington, B H 1896 'Excavations of a Roman well near Silbury Hill'. *Wiltshire Archaeol Natur Hist Mag* **29**, 166–71

Brooks, T 2002 'Prehistoric geomatics in Britain'. *Geomatics World*, May/June 2002, 26–9

Brooks, T 2006 'Geometry in the

British Stone Age'. *Mathematics Today*, April 2006, 62–5

Buchanan, A and Cossins, N 1969 *The Industrial Archaeology of the British Region*. Newton Abbot: David & Charles

Burne, C S 1915 'Scraps of folklore collected by John Philipps Emslie'. *Folklore* **26**, 153–70

Camden, W (trans) 1789 *Monumenta Britannica* (by William Camden 1607). London: T Payne

Camden, W 1806 *William Camden's Britannia* (originally published in English 1610), 2 edn Vol 3. London: John Stockdale

Cannon, J 2005 'New myths at Swallowhead: the past and the present in the landscape of the Marlborough Downs' *in* Brown, G, Field, D and McOmish, D (eds) *The Avebury Landscape: Aspects of the Field Archaeology of the Marlborough Downs*. Oxford: Oxbow, 202–11

Cannon, J and Constantine, M-A 2004 'A Welsh Bard in Wiltshire: Iolo Morganwg, Silbury and the sarsens'. *Wiltshire Archaeol Natur Hist Mag* **97**, 78–88

Charles, D K, Van Nest, J and Buikstra, J E 2004 'From the earth. Minerals and meaning in the Hopewellian world' *in* Boivin, N and Owoc, M A (eds), *Soils, Stones and Symbols: Cultural Perceptions of the Mineral World*. London: Univ College London Press, 43–70

Cleal, R 2005 '"The small compass of a grave": Early Bronze Age burial in and around Avebury and the Marlborough Downs' *in* Brown, G, Field, D and McOmish, D (eds) *The Avebury Landscape: Aspects of the Field Archaeology of the Marlborough Downs*. Oxford: Oxbow, 115–32

Clough, T H McK and Cummins, W A 1988 *Stone Axe Studies 2*. (Counc Brit Archaeol Res Rep **67**). London: Counc British Archaeol

Cope, J 1998 *The Modern Antiquarian: A Pre-millennial Odyssey through Megalithic Britain*. Hammersmith: Thorsons

Corney, M 1997 'New evidence for the Romano-British settlement by Silbury Hill'. *Wiltshire Archaeol Natur Hist Mag* **90**, 139–50

Corney, M and Walters, B 2001 'Romano-British' *in* Chadburn, A and Pomeroy-Kellinger, M (eds) *Archaeological Research Agenda for the Avebury World Heritage Site*. Salisbury: Wessex Archaeology/ English Heritage, 24–6, 47–50, 68

Cowie, J 2002 *Silbury Dawning: The Alien Visitor Gene Theory*. Edinburgh: The Media Shack.

Crittall, E (ed) 1975 *Victoria County History: A History of Wiltshire, vol 10*. Oxford: Oxford University Press

Dames, M 1976 *The Silbury Treasure: The Great Goddess Rediscovered*. London: Thames and Hudson

Dames, M 1977 *The Avebury Cycle*. London: Thames and Hudson

Darling, P 1998 'Aerial archaeology in Africa: the challenge of a continent'. *AARGnews: the newsletter of the Aerial Archaeology Research Group* **17**, 9–18

Demidoff, P 1773 'Some account of certain Tartarian antiquities. In a letter from Paul Demidoff, Esquire, at Petersburg, to Mr Peter Collinson, dated September 17, 1764'. *Archaeologia* **2**, 222–6

Devereux, P 1991 'Three-dimensional aspects of apparent relationships between selected natural and artificial features within the topography of the Avebury complex'. *Antiquity* **65**, 894–8

Douglas, J 1793 *Nenia Britannica: or a Sepulchral History of Britain*. London: Benjamin & John White

Edwards, B 2002 'A missing drawing and an overlooked text: Silbury Hill archive finds'. *Wiltshire Archaeol Natur Hist Mag* **95**, 89–92

Edwards, B 2010 'Silbury Hill: Edward Drax and the excavations of 1776'. *Wiltshire Archaeol Natur Hist Mag* **103**, 257–68

Evans, J G 1966 'A Romano-British interment in the bank of the Winterbourne, near Avebury'. *Wiltshire Archaeol Natur Hist Mag* **61**, 97–8

Field, D 2005 'Some observations on perception, consolidation and change in a land of stones' *in* Brown, G, Field, D and McOmish, D (eds) *The Avebury Landscape: Aspects of Field Archaeology in the Marlborough Downs*. Oxford: Oxbow, 87–95

Field, D 2008 *Use of Land in Central Southern England During the Neolithic and Bronze Age*. (BAR British Series 458) Oxford: Archaeopress

Fitzpatrick, A 2009 'In his hands and in his head: the Amesbury Archer as magician' *in* Clark, P (ed) *Bronze Age Connections: Cultural Contact in Prehistoric Europe*. Oxford: Oxbow, 176–88

Fowler, P 2000 *Landscape Plotted and Pieced: Landscape History and Local Archaeology in Fyfield and Overton, Wiltshire* (Soc of Antiquaries Rep **64**). London: Soc of Antiquaries

Fowler, P and Blackwell, I 1998 *The Land of Lettice Sweetapple: An English Countryside Explored*. Stroud: Tempus

Fowles, J (ed) 1980 *Monumenta Britannica by John Aubrey (1626–97) annotated by R. Legg*. Dorset: DPC

Gillings, M, Pollard, J, Wheatley, D and Peterson, R 2008 *Landscape of the Megaliths: Excavation and Fieldwork on the Avebury Monuments 1997–2003*. Oxford: Oxbow

Gingell, C 1996 'Avebury: striking a balance'. *Antiquity* **70**, 507–11

Gomme, A B 1909 'Folklore scraps from several localities'. *Folklore* **20**, 72–83

Hall, R L 1995 'Medicine Wheels, Sun Circles and the Magic of World Center Shrines' *Plains Anthropologist* **30**, 181–94

Hall, R L 1997 *An Archaeology of the Soul: North American Indian Belief and Ritual*. Illinois: University of Illinois Press

Hauser, K 2007 *Shadow Sites: Photography, Archaeology, and the British Landscape, 1927–1955*. Oxford: Oxford University Press

Hawkins, G S with White, J B 1965 *Stonehenge Decoded*. London: Doubleday

Heanley, R M 1913 'Silbury Hill'. *Folklore* **24**, 524

Hoare, R C 1821 *A History of Ancient Wiltshire 2*. London: Lackington, Hughes, Harding, Maver & Lepard

Hutton, R 2009 *Blood and Mistletoe: The History of the Druids in Britain*. Yale: Yale University Press

Irwin, J C 1982 'The sacred anthill and the cult of the primordial mound'. *History of Religions* **21**, 339–60

Iseminger, W R 2010 *Cahokia Mounds: America's First City*. Charleston, SC and London: The History Press

Jackson, J E (ed) 1862 *Wiltshire: The Topographical Collections of John Aubrey FRS Corrected and Enlarged by John Edward Jackson*. Devizes: Wiltshire Archaeol Natur Hist Society

Jones, F C and Chown, W G 1977 *History of Bristol Suburbs*. Bristol: Reece Winstone

Keiller, A 1939 'Avebury: summary of excavations, 1937 and 1938'. *Antiquity* **13**, 223–33

Latimer, J 1893 *The Annals of Bristol Vol 2*. Bath: Kingsmead Reprints

Law, L A and Crooke, W 1900 'Death and burial customs in Wiltshire'. *Folklore* **11**, 344–7

Long, W 1858 'Abury'. *Wiltshire Archaeol and Natur Hist Mag* **4**, 309–42

Lubbock, J 1865 *Pre-Historic Times, as Illustrated by Ancient Remains, and the Manners and Customs of Modern Savages*. London: Williams and Norgate

Lukis, W C (ed) 1887 *The Family Memoirs of the Rev William Stukeley MD Vol 3*. The Publications of the Surtees Society **80**

McKim, F R 1959 'An attempt to locate a burial chamber in Silbury Hill'. *Wiltshire Archaeol Natur Hist Mag* **57**, 176–8

McOmish, D, Field, D and Brown, G 1999 *The Field Archaeology of Salisbury Plain Training Area*. Swindon: English Heritage

Merewether, J 1851a 'The examination of Silbury Hill' *in* Archaeological Institute of Great Britain and Ireland *Memoirs Illustrative of the History and Antiquities of Wiltshire and the City of Salisbury. Communicated to the Annual Meeting of the Archaeological Institute of Great Britain and Ireland held at Salisbury July 1849*. London: George Bell, 73–81

Merewether, J 1851b 'Diary of the examination of barrows and other earthworks in the neighbourhood of Silbury Hill and Avebury, Wilts' *in* Archaeological Institute of Great Britain and Ireland *Memoirs Illustrative of the History and Antiquities of Wiltshire and the City of Salisbury. Communicated to the Annual Meeting of the Archaeological Institute of Great Britain and Ireland held at Salisbury July 1849*. London: George Bell, 82–11

Milner, G R 2004 T*he Moundbuilders: Ancient Peoples of Eastern North America*. London: Thames & Hudson

Mortimer, N 2003 *Stukeley Illustrated: William Stukeley's Rediscovery of Britain's Ancient Sites*. Somerset: Green Magic

Owoc, M A 2001 'The times they are a changin': experiencing continuity and development in the early Bronze Age funerary rituals of southwestern Britain' *in* Brück, J (ed) *Bronze Age Landscapes: Traditions and Transformation*. Oxford: Oxbow, 193–206

Owoc, M, A 2004 'A phenomenology of the buried landscape. Soil as material culture in the Bronze Age of south-west Britain' *in* Boivin, N and Owoc, M A *Soils, Stones and Symbols: Cultural Perceptions of the Mineral World,* London: University College London Press, 107–22

Parker Pearson, M 1993 *Bronze Age Britain.* London: Batsford

Parker Pearson, M, Chamberlain, A, Jay, M, Marshall, P, Pollard, J, Richards, C, Thomas, J, Tilley, C and Welham K 2009 'Who was buried at Stonehenge?'. *Antiquity* **83**, 23–39

Parslew, P 2004 *Beckhampton: Time Present and Time Past.* East Knoyle: Hobnob Press

Pass, A C 1887 'Recent explorations at Silbury Hill'. *Wiltshire Archaeol Natur Hist Mag* **23**, 245–54

Passmore, A D 1920 'Silbury Hill'. *Wiltshire Archaeol Natur Hist Mag* **41**, 185–6

Petrie, F W M 1924 'Report of the diggings in Silbury Hill, August 1922'. *Wiltshire Archaeol Natur Hist Mag* **42**, 215–18

Pitts, M 2009 'My Archaeology'. *British Archaeology* **105**, March/April 2009

Pollard, J and Cleal, R M J 2004 'Dating Avebury' *in* Cleal, R M J and Pollard, J (eds) *Monuments and Material Culture: Papers in Honour of an Avebury Archaeologist: Isobel Smith.* Salisbury: Hobnob Press, 120–9

Pollard, J and Reynolds, A 2002 *Avebury: The Biography of a Landscape.* Stroud: Tempus

Powell, A B, Allen, M J and Barnes, I 1996 *Archaeology in the Avebury Area, Wiltshire: Recent Discoveries along the Line of the Kennet Valley Foul Sewer Pipeline, 1993.* (Wessex Archaeology Rep **8**). Salisbury: Wessex Archaeology

Pugh, R P (ed) 1965 *Victoria County History: A History of Wiltshire Vol 8.* Oxford: Oxford University Press

Quennell, M and Quennell, C H B 1907 *Everyday Life in the New Stone Age, Bronze and Early Iron Ages.* London: Batsford

Rawlins, M 1999 *Butcher, Baker, Saddlemaker: Village Life in Avebury from 1920 to 1974.* Chippenham: Anthony Rowe

Renfrew, C 1973 'Monuments, mobilization and social organization in Neolithic Wessex' *in* Renfrew, C *The Explanation of Culture Change: Models in Prehistory.* London: Duckworth, 539–58.

Reynolds, A 2001 'Avebury: a Late Anglo-Saxon burh?'. *Antiquity* **75**, 29–30

Reynolds, A 2005 'From *pagus* to parish: territory and settlement in the Avebury region from the late Roman period to the Domesday Survey' *in* Brown, G, Field, D and McOmish, D (eds) *The Avebury Landscape: Aspects of Field Archaeology of the Marlborough Downs.* Oxford: Oxbow, 164–80

Richards, C 1996a 'Monuments as landscape: creating the centre of the world in late Neolithic Orkney'. *World Archaeology* **28** (2), 190–208

Richards C 1996b 'Henges and water: towards an elemental understanding of monumentality and landscape in late Neolithic

Britain'. *Journal of Material Culture* **1**, 313–36

Robinson, M 1997 'The insects' *in* Whittle, A *Sacred Mound Holy Rings. Silbury Hill and the West Kennet Palisade Enclosures: A Later Neolithic complex in North Wiltshire* (Cardiff Studies in Archaeol. Oxbow Monogr **74**). Oxford: Oxbow 36–47

Robinson, P 1992 'Some Late Saxon mounts from Wiltshire'. *Wiltshire Archaeol Natur Hist Mag* **85**, 63–9

Scarre, C 2004 'Choosing stones, remembering places. Geology and intention in the megalithic monuments of Western Europe' *in* Boivin, N and Owoc, M A *Soils, Stones and Symbols: Cultural Perceptions of the Mineral World.* London: University College London Press, 187–202

Simmonds, S (ed) 2008 *Avebury World Heritage Site: Values and Voices.* Wiltshire: Kennet District Council

Słupecki, L P 2006 'Large burial mounds of Cracow' *in* Šmejda, L (ed.) *Archaeology of Burial Mounds.* University West Bohemia: Plze, 119–42

Smith, A C 1862 'Silbury'. *Wiltshire Archaeol Natur Hist Mag* **7**, 145–91

Smith, A C 1884 *Guide to the British and Roman Antiquities of the North Wiltshire Downs.* Devizes: WAHNS

Stukeley, W 1743 *Stonehenge: A Temple Restor'd to the British Druids and, Abury, a Temple of the British Druids.* London: printed by W Innys and R Mamby

Swanton, M (trans) (2000) *The Anglo-Saxon Chronicles.* London: Phoenix Press

Taylor, H 1951 'The Tynings Farm barrow group: third report'. *Proc University of Bristol Spelaeological Society* **6**, 111–73

Tilley, C 1994 *A Phenomenology of Landscape: Places, Paths and Monuments.* Oxford: Berg

Topping, P 2010 'Native American mound building traditions' *in* Leary, J, Darvill, T and Field, D (eds) *Round Mounds and Monumentality in the British Neolithic and Beyond.* (Neolithic Studies Group Seminar Papers). Oxford: Oxbow, 219–52

Toulmin Smith, L (ed) 1964 *The Itinerary of John Leland, vol 5.* London: Centaur Press

Tucker, C 1851 'Report of the examination of Silbury Hill' *in* Archaeological Institute of Great Britain and Ireland *Memoirs Illustrative of the History and Antiquities of Wiltshire and the City of Salisbury. Communicated to the Annual Meeting of the Archaeological Institute of Great Britain and Ireland held at Salisbury July 1849.* London: George Bell, 297–303

Ucko, P J, Hunter, M, Clark, A and David, A 1991 *Avebury Reconsidered: From the 1660s to the 1990s.* London: Unwin Hyman

Wainwright, G J 1971 'The excavation of a Late Neolithic enclosure at Marden, Wiltshire'. *Antiquaries Journal* **51**, 177–239

Wakefield, J D 1999 *Legendary Landscapes: Secrets of Ancient Wiltshire Revealed.* Marlborough: Nod Press

Welfare, H 1989 'John Aubrey – the

first archaeological surveyor?'
in Bowden, M, Mackay, D and
Topping, P (eds) *From Cornwall to
Caithness: Aspects of British Field
Archaeology.* (BAR British Ser 209).
Oxford: Archaeopress, 17–28

Wells, H G 1922 (2006 edn) *The
Secret Places of the Heart*. Fairfield:
1stworldlibrary.com

Whittle, A 1997 *Sacred Mound Holy
Rings: Silbury Hill and the West
Kennet Palisade Enclosures: A Later
Neolithic Complex in North Wiltshire*
(Cardiff Studies in Archaeol. Oxbow
Monogr **74**). Oxford: Oxbow

Whittle, A, Pollard, J and Grigson,C
1999 *The Harmony of Symbols*.
Oxford: Oxbow

Wilkinson, J 1869 'A report of
diggings made in Silbury Hill, and
in the ground adjoining'. *Wiltshire
Archaeol Natur Hist Mag* **11**, 113–18

Woodward, S L and McDonald, J N
2002 *Indian Mounds of the Middle
Ohio Valley: A Guide to Mounds and
Earthworks of the Adena, Hopewell,
Cole, and Fort Ancient People*.
Virginia, Blacksburg: The McDonald
& Woodward Publishing Company

Youngs, S 1998 'Medieval hanging
bowls from Wiltshire'. *Wiltshire
Archaeol Natur Hist Mag* **91**, 35–41

Index

Index

Reconstruction drawings as imagined by Judith Dobie

Photographs by James O Davies pp xviii (DP100304), 26, 88 (DP054780), 114 (DP054505),
142, 143, 145, 147, 151, 152 (DP059781), 158, 167, 169, 172 (DP100305); David Field 126, 127,
Damian Grady 6, 46 (24814/002), 72, 130 (24861/005); Ellie Leary 92 (bottom); Jim Leary
110, 133, 178, 179; Ian Leonard 68 (DP039024), 80, 81, 82, 85; Fachtna McAvoy 105; Sarah May
125; Andy Payne 154; Duncan Stirk 14, 92 (top), 93, 103, 168

Height data pp 7, 137, 141; aerial photography p 160: Licensed to English Heritage for PGA,
through NextPerspectives™

SRTM data courtesy of the CGIAR Consortium for Spatial Information: pp 4, 148

Index